POPE FRANCIS'
SPIRITUALITY
and Our Story

POPE FRANCIS'
SPIRITUALITY
and
Our Story

Robert E. Lauder

Resurrection Press
An Imprint of
CATHOLIC BOOK PUBLISHING CORP.
Totowa • New Jersey

First published in April, 2014
Catholic Book Publishing/Resurrection Press
77 West End Road
Totowa, NJ 07512

ISBN 978-1-933066-17-2

Cover design by Geoffrey Butz

Printed in the United States of America

www.catholicbookpublishing.com

2 3 4 5 6 7 8 9 10

Dedication

This book is dedicated to
Brigid Sophia Sullivan.
May her story be filled with
faith, hope and love.

Acknowledgments

Grateful acknowledgment is made
to *The Brooklyn Tablet* for
material which appeared previously in its pages
and to Emilie Cerar of Resurrection Press
whose guidance and encouragement
in bringing this book to publication
have been greatly appreciated.
I also wish to express my gratitude to Iris Flores,
a wonderful friend without whose dedication,
kindness, and patience this book would never
have been written.

Contents

Introduction

Story: Divine and Human

M Y reflections in this book are personal but I hope not private. As I try to share my reflections on God's gift of story I am hoping that they will be as meaningful and important to readers as they are to me. The chapters on "The Power of Story" and "God in Film" have grown out of my experience in the last fifty years of being profoundly influenced by Catholic novels and by films that either directly or indirectly reveal the mystery of God. In the last fifty years I have read or re-read over one hundred and fifty Catholic novels for an adult education course that I teach, and have viewed more than two hundred and fifty classic or near classic films because of film festivals that I have conducted. Chapters Four and Five are intended to speak both to those familiar with Catholic novels and those who are lovers of movies, but also, to introduce others to the mystery and marvel of great stories, whether they appear on the written page or on a movie screen. Pope Francis has written the following:

> *"Dialogue is born from a respectful attitude toward the other person, from a conviction that the other person has something good to say. It supposes that we can make room in our heart for their point of view, their opinion and their proposals. Dialogue entails a warm reception and not a preemptive con-*

*demnation. To dialogue, one must know how to lower
the defenses, to open the doors of one's home and to
offer warmth."* [1]

This book is an attempt at dialogue. In writing it, I have
tried to dialogue with some contemporary theologians
and philosophers and with Pope Francis. I am hoping that
my efforts in writing this book might help others in their
dialogue with God. I do not know Pope Francis personally but from the moment of the announcement of his election on Wednesday, March 13, 2013, I have followed his
papacy closely. I cannot recall anyone making such a
strong impression on so many in such a short time. It is
easy to chronicle events in the opening days of his papacy. In the foreword to Matthew Bunson's *Pope Francis*,
Greg Erlandson writes the following:

> *"His first words were softly enunciated:* 'Buona
> sera' *('Good Evening'). It was almost casual, certain-
> ly informal, yet a small sign that we were about to
> meet a man quite different from some of our expecta-
> tions. Think of those first moments and the other spon-
> taneous signs he gave that revealed to us evidence of
> his character: He prayed for his predecessor, Benedict,
> 'the emeritus bishop of Rome,' using the basic prayers
> of our Catholic faith. He asked us to bless him before
> he blessed us. He refused to wear the more ornate
> papal vestments. And he insistently presented himself
> as the bishop and pastor of Rome.*
> *"There was humility to his very first words and
> actions that not only captured the imagination of the*

---

[1] Jorge Mario Bergoglio and Abraham Skorka. *On Heaven and Earth.* Translated by
Alejandro Bermudez and Howard Goodman. (New York: Image, 2013), p. XIV.

crowd in the Saint Peter's Square, but also the tens of millions watching on television. In the days that followed, he did not so much outline a program as reveal aspects of his character. Some of these gestures—blessing a pregnant woman outside of the Basilica of Saint Mary Major, paying his own bill at the hotel where he had been staying, embracing the crippled man in Saint Peter's Square, choosing to celebrate Holy Thursday with young people in a juvenile detention center—dramatically attracted the attention of the world. It is not as if no pope had ever done these things. Yet the fact that he was at once both forceful and humble—insisting that he be able to do these things from the very beginning—entranced the media and fed the popular imagination. At the same time, if we focus only on the empathetic gesture and the sympathetic act, we only understand part of Pope Francis. While he has not laid out his program yet—and may not for some time as he adjusts to both the Vatican and the global complexities of a world Church—there are clues to who the man is and what he considers priorities." [2]

Father Mitch Pacwa, S.J., expressing his joy that a fellow Jesuit had become the first member of the Society of Jesus to be elected Pope, after commenting on the Pope's remarks from the balcony mentions the following:

"This moment was followed by many small moments of making ordinary actions quite uncommon—riding a bus with the cardinals, praying

---

[2] Greg Erlandson, Foreword to Matthew Bunson, *Pope Francis*, (Huntington Indiana, 2013), pp. 11-12.

*alone at Saint Mary Major, stopping to pay his bill
in person at a Rome hotel for priests, calling the man
who delivered his papers in Buenos Aires to cancel
the subscription, meeting with the Jesuit Father
General Adolfo Nicolás, S.J., to accept his offer of
Jesuit support to the new pope, and the Pope's exten-
sion of his apostolic blessing to all Jesuits and those
who work with them. These moments stream forth
from him, making his office yet more amazing."* [3]

In writing the stories of our life, we can be helped or
hindered by others. I believe that Pope Francis is a
prophetic powerful witness to the deepest meaning of
the human story, a voice that can challenge us and
remind us of the most important truths about God and
about ourselves. By his words and actions before and
since becoming the Bishop of Rome, Pope Francis has
delivered a unified message. Most of the Pope's statements referred to in this book were made before he was
elected Pope, but the vision in them corresponds to
what he has said since his election. For example, his first
encyclical is an inspiring example of the Pope's vision of
the poverty of the human person, a poverty enriched by
a relationship with Christ. A spirituality has been
revealed.

The following lines from the encyclical *Lumen Fidei*
could serve as a summary statement of the Pope's
vision:

*"In God's gift of faith, a supernatural infused
virtue, we realize that a great love has been offered*

---

[3] Mitch Pacwa, Foreword in Andrea Tornelli, *Francis: Pope of a New World* (San
Francisco: Ignatius Press, 2013), p. xii.

us, a good word has been spoken to us, and that when we welcome that word, Jesus Christ the Word made flesh, the Holy Spirit transforms us, lights up our way to the future and enables us joyfully to advance along that way on wings of hope. Thus wonderfully interwoven, faith, hope and charity are the driving force of the Christian life as it advances towards full communion with God." [4]

One senses a kind of urgency in The Holy Father's encyclical. Pope Francis wants culture to be transformed.

"Our culture has lost its sense of God's tangible presence and activity in our world. We think that God is to be found in the beyond, on another level of reality, far removed from our everyday relationships. But if this were the case, if God could not act in the world, His love would not be truly powerful, truly real, and thus not even true, a love capable of delivering the bliss that it promises. It would make no difference at all whether we believed in Him or not. Christians, on the contrary, profess their faith in God's tangible and powerful love which really does act in history and determines its final destiny: a love that can be encountered, a love fully revealed in Christ's Passion, Death and Resurrection." [5]

The Holy Father believes deeply in the presence of the Holy Spirit in everyone's life.

"Because faith is a way, it also has to do with the lives of those men and women who, though not

---

[4] Francis, Encyclical Letter, *Lumen Fidei*. (Vatican: Libreria Editrice Vaticana, 2013), section 7.
[5] *Ibid.*, section 17.

believers, nonetheless desire to believe and continue to seek. To the extent that they are sincerely open to love and set out with whatever light they can find, they are already, even without knowing it, on the path leading to faith. They strive to act as if God existed, at times because they realize how important He is for finding a sure compass for our life in common or because they experience a desire for light amid darkness, but also because in perceiving life's grandeur and beauty they intuit that the presence of God would make it all the more beautiful. Saint Irenaeus of Lyons tells how Abraham, before hearing God's voice, had already sought Him 'in the ardent desire of his heart' and 'went throughout the whole world, asking himself where God was to be found,' until 'God had pity on him who, all alone, had sought Him in silence.' Anyone who sets off on the path of doing good to others is already drawing near to God, is already sustained by His help, for it is characteristic of the Divine Light to brighten our eyes whenever we walk towards the fullness of love." [6]

In this book, I attempt to use Pope Francis' spirituality to emphasize and highlight the meaning and mystery of the human story, the gifts that God has given us to live unselfishly, perhaps even heroically.

---

[6] *Ibid.*, section 35.

Chapter 1

God: Giver of Gifts

I AM starting to write this book shortly after engaging in centering prayer. Part of centering prayer is being silent with God, giving God time to speak to you. I now feel compelled to try to say what I mean by urging people to listen to God. Often centering prayer ends with the person just enjoying God's presence. While the person praying may be silent, I believe that God is speaking.

In recent years, I have become very aware of people not listening. I am surprised how often people interrupt one another. Just a few days ago, I gave a lecture and I said something that apparently disturbed someone in the audience. When the person publicly disagreed with what she thought I had said, I tried to explain what I meant. Each time I tried, the person interrupted. She seemed unable to listen to me. She thought she knew what my statement meant and though I tried to explain to her that it did not mean what she thought it meant, my effort was in vain. This is not an isolated incident in my experience. Often I find that in a private conversation I am interrupted in the middle of some statement that I am trying to make. Whether others have the same experience of being interrupted in conversations I do not know, but I wonder if one of the reasons that people might have for not listening is that all of us are under various pressures and many of us live at a very hectic pace.

The importance of listening to God has become more central in my own understanding of the Christian life. Reading a number of contemporary theologians has also convinced me that one of the problems that makes religion irrelevant to many people today is that people cannot be still, cannot reflect on what is most important in life. Though I can try to help students at St. John's University to be more reflective through the study of philosophy, and though I can try in homilies and columns in the Catholic press to call people to personal reflection, I keep hoping for some magical solution that will impress upon some of my contemporaries the importance of living an examined life, the importance of personal reflection upon how and why they are living as they are. Of course I also have to remind myself to be more reflective. Pope Francis has said:

> *"What every person must be told is to look inside himself. Distraction is an interior fracture. It will never lead the person to encounter himself for it impedes him from looking in the mirror of his heart."* [7]

When I say that at times when we are praying we should be silent and listen to God I do not mean that we are going to hear a voice. That has never happened to me. What I mean when I say that God will speak to us is that in our silence God will communicate with us. In centering prayer we are not present to God to make petitions nor

---

[7] Bergoglio and Skorka, op. cit., p.3.

are we present to God to tell God our problems. In centering prayer we try to be present to God Who is always present to us in a way similar to how two friends might be present to one another.

One of the problems that I have had in praying is that I have tended to think of God as statically present to me, almost like an observer, a disinterested onlooker. I tend to think of God as an onlooker. Of course this is a false view of God. In our lives God is actively present. When we pray God is not just a listener. In fact we could not even pray except that God calls us, touches us, invites us. The gift of grace enables us to turn to God. So God is active even before we become active, even before we raise our minds and hearts toward God.

I believe that God wants all of us to enter more deeply into the love relationship that God has initiated with us. Perhaps if we are silent in the presence of God, we will be able to hear how this God is calling us into this deeper relationship. It might be through some insight we receive into ourselves when we are silent before God, or it might be through some insight we receive into the mystery of God when we are silent in God's presence. I cannot predict how God will communicate with any of us, not even with me, but though I cannot predict how God will communicate in our silence, I believe we should be very confident that God will communicate.

When I studied undergraduate philosophy many years ago as a seminarian, though I was very interested in the subject, much of what was taught went over my head. It was years later when I studied theology and still later when I did graduate studies in philosophy that some of what had been taught to me when I was an undergraduate began to make sense. In a perfect world, college students, at least those who are seventeen or eighteen years of age, could postpone their studies in philosophy for a few years. They would profit if they studied philosophy in their late twenties or even early thirties. Then the questions that philosophy poses and tries to answer might be more meaningful to them. Alas, it is not a perfect world and students have to get a college degree quickly so that they can take the next step in their studies or in their careers.

One of the great insights of traditional metaphysics, at least the metaphysics based on St. Thomas Aquinas' thought, is that God does not love us because we are lovable. God's love is literally creative. When God loves, being appears. God's love brings us into existence, God's love makes us be, and makes us attractive and lovable. God cannot create anything that does not in some way resemble God. Even creatures that do not seem very attractive to us, such as tarantulas and cockroaches, resemble God because they exist, because they share in God's being. But among the creatures within our experience in this world, human persons resemble God more than any other creatures.

Any serious reflection on the truth that God has freely chosen to create each of us should lead to a sense of awe and wonder and to some appreciation of our dignity, value, and importance. Out of billions and billions of possible human beings, really an unlimited number of possible human beings that God could have created, God chose to create me. God did not merely create me as a part of some large group in a kind of assembly line fashion. God freely chose to create me, the unique human being that I am. Every person reading this book can make the same statement. God's freely loving us brought us into being, into existence. That truth is awesome.

It was probably on a Cursillo that I first heard the statement "God does not make junk!" God cannot make anything that is not beautiful. This is the ultimate reason why inferiority complexes are so false and poor self-images are so erroneous. God's love for us, which brought us into existence and which is constant, should help us to see our very existence as a gift. None of us had to exist. Each of us is the result of God's freely given love. If God's love were ever withdrawn, we could cease to be. If for one second God stopped loving me, I would be a part of the greatest disappearing act in history! We will never be able to list God's gifts to us. Everything we have and every blessing we have received is ultimately due to God. There is no counting or numbering God's gifts. Still I find it helpful to focus on God's creative act of love that has brought us into existence.

One of the courses in philosophy that I teach every spring semester at St. John's University is about the mystery of God. Early in the course, I emphasize to the students that, because God is the greatest mystery of all, nothing crystal clear can be said about God, nor can any statements about God be adequate. This does not mean that there can be no true statements about God but only that all statements about God are going to be incomplete. No matter what we say about God we can always add that God is more than what we conceive God to be. We are never going to fit the Infinite God into our finite minds in such a way that we can say that we clearly understand God. It is because God is always greater than we think that God will always be mysterious to us. We will never understand God the way that God understands God. In fact we will never know anything the way that God knows.

A book that has helped me to see more deeply into the mystery of God is Michael J. Himes' *Doing the Truth in Love: Conversations about God, Relationships and Service.* It is not only one of the best books in theology that I have read in the last twenty years. I think it is one of the best books in theology that I have ever read. After stressing that all statements about God are more or less inadequate, Father Himes suggests a way of thinking of God that is better than all others or, to put it his way, is the least inadequate way of speaking about God. Himes writes:

> *"What the Christian tradition maintains is the least inadequate expression for God finds its clearest, sharpest, simplest statement in one of the last-written documents of the collection of early Christian documents which we call the New Testament, the first letter of John. There we read that 'God is Love' (1 John 4:8 and 16). But the love which is offered as the least wrong way to think and speak about God is of a very peculiar sort:* agape. Agape *is a Greek word meaning love which is purely other-directed, love which seeks no return, love which does not want anything back. Perhaps, so as not to confuse it with the many other meanings which we attach to the word 'love' in English, we might translate* agape *'pure self-gift.' "* [8]

Father Himes has convinced me that thinking of God as "pure self-gift" is the best way to think of God, and I

---

[8] Michael Himes, *Doing the Truth in Love: Conversations About God, Relationships and Service* (New York: Paulist Press, 1995), pp. 9-10.

am surprised that this beautiful idea of God has come to me so late in my life. This may be due to harsh images of God that were taught to me in my early religious training, taught by people who sincerely believed those images were true. It may be due to the lack of emphasis on God as love when I was studying as a seminarian. Perhaps it may also be due to a fear that if we emphasize that God is love we may think that this frees us of any obligations toward God or to living as Christians.

While thinking of God as pure self-gift may be the least inadequate way of thinking of God, it does not make living a Christian life less demanding. Being loved by God does not have to be earned or merited or won because God's love for us is a gift but it does call for a response from us. While there are very soft, sentimental and saccharine views of love in our society, real love, the kind of love that is called for by God's love for us, is demanding. Being unselfish always involves a sacrifice and most of us do not find making sacrifices easy.

What has especially impressed me as I have come to see God as pure self-gift is that nothing we do can stop God from loving us. God's commitment to us is for eternity. Even if we sin seriously or gravely, God does not stop loving us. By our sin we may make it difficult for God's love to influence us but we have not forced God to stop loving us. Even those persons in hell, if there are any persons in hell, are loved by God. All those who present us with gifts are imitating God as pure self-gift.

I intend this book to call attention to the profound truth, especially relevant today, that God has placed us in a deeply meaningful world. We are not adrift in a chaotic universe that has no pattern or direction to it. Through his insights into the process of evolution, theologian John Haught [9] has argued persuasively that the universe has a story and that the narrative pattern discoverable through science can be interpreted as pointing toward some future fulfillment. My Christian faith tells me that God is the absolute future calling creation into an exciting future and that we are part of that story, capable of a profound personal relationship with God and with one another. In our stories, each of us is on a path with God. Pope Francis has spoken eloquently about God's involvement in our lives:

> *"What a great word: path! In my personal experience with God I cannot do without the path. I would say that one encounters God walking, moving, seeking Him and allowing oneself to be sought by Him. They are two paths that meet. On one hand, there is our path that seeks Him, driven by that instinct that flows from the heart; and after, when we have encountered each other, we realize that He was the one who had been searching for us from the start. The initial religious experience is that of walking: walk to the land that I am going to give you. It is a promise that God makes to Abraham. In that promise, in this, in this walking, an alliance is established that consolidates over time. Because of this I say that my experience with God takes place along the path, both in the search and in allowing myself to be sought, even if it may be by diverse paths—of pain, of joy, of light, or of darkness."* [10]

What we think of God deeply influences how we think of ourselves and how we think of ourselves greatly influ-

---

[9] John Haught, *Science and Religion: From Conflict to Conversation* (New York: Paulist Press, 1995), pp. 162-182.

[10] Bergoglio and Skorka, *op. cit.*, p. 2.

ences our image of God. I think that this applies to our image of God as gift-giver and to our images of ourselves as gift-givers. In giving we imitate God, we mirror God's unselfishness and love.

Writing on gift has caused me to remember many of the gifts that I have received in my life. If there is any pattern that my memories follow I don't know what that pattern is. For example for some reason unknown to me as I started to write this book, I thought of a Christmas that my family celebrated when I was in the fifth or sixth grade. Every Christmas when my sister and I came down from our bedrooms to see what was left under the tree for us, we found what seemed like a countless number of gifts. This particular Christmas, I found a new football. All the other gifts taken together could not compare in my estimation to the football. I can recall my mother joking to my father "We could have saved a lot of money by just buying the ball!"

More than sixty years later, I still can recreate in my memory the smell of the new cowhide and the feel of the ball in my hand as I raised my arm as though I was going to throw a forward pass in our living room. When I received that gift years ago, I was excited about the ball. Now as I recall the experience, I am deeply touched as I imagine the love that moved my parents to know that this gift would be special to me. When we realize that the giver has spent time and effort trying to choose a gift that would really please us, the gift assumes a new importance because it obviously represents the giver's love for us. Every gift, at least to some extent, represents the giver and says something about the giver.

There are times in life, I think the Thanksgiving holiday is one of them, when some people try to list the gifts they have received from God. Often the list includes family, friends, health, employment and perhaps some special material possessions such as a house or automobile. But the greatest gift that God has offered to every human person is God. All other gifts, even family and friends, are wonderful because they are images of God. Their goodness and beauty are real because they mirror God's goodness and beauty. All blessings are like mirrors of God. Any gift or blessing that we receive that is not God, as wonderful as the gift and blessing might be, will never satisfy us because we are made for God and nothing less than God will fulfill us. Every gift that God gives, and ultimately all gifts are due to God's graciousness, is a sign of God's love for us but the greatest sign of God's love is God inviting us into an intimate love relationship. If one of the best ways to think of God is to think of God as pure self-gift, then when we offer gifts we are imitating God. Even though we will never love exactly as God loves, and none of us will ever be pure self-gift, the ability to be a gift-giver is itself one of the great gifts we have received. Even the capacity to love freely is a gift from God. Pope Francis has stressed the all-encompassing love of God:

> *"God makes Himself felt in the heart of each person . . . He calls everyone. He moves everyone to seek Him and to discover Him through creation. In our case, that of Judaism and Christianity, we have a personal revelation. God Himself encounters us; He reveals Himself to us, He shows us the way and He accompanies us; He tells us His name, He guides us through the prophets. Christians believe, ultimately, that He*

manifested Himself to us and gave Himself to us through Jesus Christ." [11]

All Is Grace, All Is Gift

Meditating on death as a gift, I re-read Gerard Manley Hopkins' poem "The Wreck of the Deutschland." When I was a student in college, the priest who taught English Literature told me that if some day I could read and understand Hopkins' masterpiece, I might benefit from it as much as from any "spiritual reading." His statement surprised me. Probably at that time in my life I tended to separate poetry, novels, plays, and films from what I thought of as reading that a person did in order to grow closer to God. I am no longer comfortable with such a separation. Years after college I took a course on Hopkins and I now think I understand the main theme of the poem, which is one of the most basic and profound mysteries of the Christian faith. If I had to state the theme of Hopkins' poem briefly, I probably would express it as "All is grace." This is a statement made by Saint Thérèse, The Little Flower. It is also the line that ends George Bernanos' marvelous novel *The Diary of a Country Priest*. The events that led up to Hopkins writing the poem were the Falk laws in Germany that forced five Catholic nuns to flee their country of birth. The ship, the Deutschland, that was supposed to carry them to safety, was wrecked in a storm. Hopkins views the tragedy with the eyes of faith and sees the presence of the Risen Christ in the storm. What may appear to a non-believer as a total tragedy is a gift from God to the sisters. The nuns don't need to seek the mercy of God because the merciful Lord is coming to meet them.

---

[11] *Ibid.*, p. 19.

The best essay that I have read on the poem was written by Peter Quinn. Entitled "The Catholic Imagination," the essay appears in Quinn's wonderful book *Looking for Jimmy: A Search for Irish America*. Early in his essay Quinn comments on how their Catholic background greatly influenced the consciousness and conscience of playwright Eugene O'Neill and novelist James Joyce though both men would probably describe themselves as nonbelievers. Quinn is not suggesting that somehow O'Neill and Joyce remained "closet-Catholics" but rather that it may have been easier for these two artists to get out of the Church than to get the Church out of them. Their Catholic background shows in much of what they wrote. Dealing with some of the images in Father Hopkins' poem Quinn writes the following:

> *"In the poem, Hopkins uses the word mercy five times, a clear allusion to the five wounds of Jesus' passion:* Five! The finding and sake/and cipher of suffering Christ. *This is neither a cipher to be decoded nor a mystery to be solved, but a truth that can only be denied or accepted. For me, the whole Catholic faith and imagination springs from this acceptance, this reconciliation of worldliness and holiness embodied in the Incarnation and consummated on the cross that makes us givers and receivers of mercy, both. And once accepted, how is it possible for the Catholic imagination not to embrace and explore the human condition honestly, to seek God in one another, in our nobility and squalor, in our infinite ability to break each other's hearts."* [12]

[12] Peter Quinn, *Looking for Jimmy: A Search for Irish America* (New York: The Overlook Press, 2007), pp. 185-186.

Quinn suggests that in his poem Father Hopkins imagines a "metaphysic of mercy." As much as anything that I have written on "gift" the notion of "metaphysic of mercy" sums up what I have been trying to communicate about God as "pure self-gift." We don't have to search for God as though God is absent from our lives and we don't have to beg God as though we have to persuade God to be on our side. Quinn concludes his essay with the following statement:

> "And here in this time of division in the Church, of corruption and suspicion and scandal, if I had to choose one part of the Catholic imagination for Catholics to cherish and explore and, above all, to make part of our dealings with the world and one another, it would be the merciful Christ of whom Hopkins sings to us: Our passion-plunged giant risen . . . Let him Easter in us." [13]

The only response that I can think of making to Quinn's comment is Alleluia! Alleluia! Alleluia!

Imitating God: Giving Our Self

A priest friend of mine once told me that he thought that all entertainers should go straight to heaven. When I heard this statement I did not agree with it but I do think that now I have a better understanding of it. I suspect he thought that entertainers gave so freely of themselves for the sake of others' enjoyment that they deserved heaven.

Essential to loving is not what talents the lover has. Of course when we love someone or some group of persons we want to share whatever gifts or talents we have with

---

[13] *Ibid.*, p. 187.

those we love. However the talent is not the love. I think that human loving mirrors God's love. God is pure self-gift. When a human person loves, he or she freely makes a self-gift to the beloved. Whatever talents the lover has or does not have is secondary. What is most important, what is primary, is that the person offers himself or herself to the beloved. Any expression we use to express this self-gift is awkward but I like the expressions "I am for you" or "I am at your service" or "I am available to you and for you." It is the free gift of self that is the basic component of every act of love.

Of course there are different ways of expressing this gift of self and there are various ways of loving. A married man does not love his next door neighbor the way he loves his wife. Love can be expressed by holding a door for someone or by forgiving someone or by making a life commitment to someone.

Depending on the number of loving relationships a person has, love can be very demanding. If a person tells me that he has one close friend, I would say he is greatly blessed. If he tells me he has fifteen close friends, I would doubt his statement. Close friendships take time and effort and presence. One of the most giving persons I have ever known, a professor who was a genius and a very loving man, was a person whom everyone wanted to know better. I once heard him say that he felt that people were "eating" him. We only have a limited amount of time and energy.

While offering your self in some way as a gift to others can be demanding even exhausting, lovers discover that they are at their best when they are giving themselves away. This is a great paradox: we grow and develop and find special happiness when we focus on others, give ourselves to others, love others. Loving helps lovers grow and develop as persons. The basic vocation of every person, a vocation offered to us by God, is to be a lover. Loving makes us like God. The great Jewish philosopher, Martin Buber, was correct when he described love as the godly in existence.

Not only do people have the opportunity to grow and develop through loving. *Being loved* is one of the great gifts in life. I suggest that those who love us can actually "create" us. Of course they do not create us the way that God creates us. God creates from nothing. Lovers through the power of their self-gift can help those they love to grow and develop in ways that might not have happened without the experience of being loved. People who love can be more creative than the greatest artists. Great artists make beautiful objects. Lovers can make beautiful people. For people to be changed through being loved, it is necessary that the beloved accept the love of the lover What is it that loving and being loved could never accomplish? I cannot answer that question.

Hopkins' Selves

My favorite poem is Gerard Manley Hopkins' #34, often identified by the first four words of the poem: "As kingfishers catch fire." In the poem, Hopkins portrays each being as dynamically speaking itself. It is as though each created being has a message to tell and that message is itself. Four lines of the poem are:

> *"Each mortal thing does one thing and the same:*
> *Deals out that being indoors each one dwells.*

Selves-goes itself; myself it speaks and spells,
Crying What I do is me: for that I came." [14]

Reading Hopkins' poem I think of every finite being in our experience—trees, plants, animals, persons—as "messages from God or words from God." Each finite being has something to tell us by its very nature. It speaks itself. Martin Buber thought that each being had both a passive aspect and an active aspect. The passive aspect enables us to characterize the being, perhaps to put it into a class, to understand it as one of many, perhaps to define it or at least to describe it. The active aspect is less easy to understand. I think of it as though each being was reaching out to us, almost trying to tell us something, trying to reveal to us something about itself or even about its Creator. If my way of thinking about beings is correct then everything that God has created is a gift to us from God. I suppose the mystics recognize this more than the rest of us and this may be why they are mystics. Thinking of all of creation as gift makes everything precious and sacred.

This way of looking at creation fits in nicely with our belief in the Resurrection of Jesus and our own resurrection. That Jesus conquered sin and death through His crucifixion and resurrection changes everything. All of creation has been redeemed. In relation to us, God is gift-giver. The most wonderful gift is His Son but everything we experience is gift. Some poets may have a sense of this and I suspect that the saints have a strong sense of it. I think of poet William Blake's line about seeing the world in a grain of sand and eternity in an hour. That created beings can speak to us of their Creator is possible because

---

[14] Gerard Manley Hopkins #34 in *Gerard Manley Hopkins: A Selection of His Poems and Prose* by W. H. Gardner (London: The Penguin Press, 1953), p. 54.

of Jesus' Resurrection. Everything is different because of that event. Any good that is done, any growth in our relationship with God, any acts of unselfishness that we do are due to the profound and liberating truth that our relationship with God has become possible because of Jesus' Resurrection.

The mystery of Resurrection tells us not only about Jesus but also about ourselves. Risen life is what we are journeying toward and it will be the marvelous culmination to all our efforts to follow Christ. Our lives are adventures in grace. This is true of every person, even of those who profess no religious faith. The Risen Lord is the companion of all persons on their journey in this world. The relationship with the Risen Lord, which begins on earth, will reach its fulfillment beyond the grave. Another way of saying this is that the final union with the Risen Lord is the ultimate gift, reached through an adventurous journey that was filled with gifts from God. Our lives on earth are an ongoing dialogue with God. Not so much a dialogue with words as with actions: God offers gifts which in some way represent God Himself and we accept gratefully and respond by the way we live. Our lives are like an ongoing Eucharist: God loves us and invites us into a love relationship and we say "Yes" to God's self-gift and try to live out the implications of our relationship with God. Reflecting on God's love for us, Pope Francis said:

> *"John said: 'In this is love: not that we have loved God, but that he loved us . . . We love because he first loved us.' For me, if the religious experience doesn't have this* measure of astonishment, of surprise, if this compassion is not sprung upon you—*then*

*it's cold, it doesn't draw us in completely; it's a differ-
ent kind of experience that doesn't bring us to a tran-
scendental plane. Though we all know that living this
kind of transcendentalism today is difficult, due to the
dizzy rhythm of life, the fast pace of change, and the
lack of a long-term view. However, oases are very
important to the religious experience. . . . The encounter with God must come surging from within. I
must put myself in the presence of God and, aided by
His Word, go forward in what He desires."* [15]

The Dynamism of Love

A friend once questioned me about my insistence that
God loves us and that we don't have to win or merit or
earn that love, that it is pure gift. She thought that I was
implicitly giving people the license to sin because no matter what they did, nothing could stop God from loving
them. Her remark set me thinking about living as a
Christian and about how we should experience the
Christian life. Her remark also set me thinking about the
experience of conversion.

In my own experience, I have come across two ways
that people think about Christian morality that miss the
mark. One way is to think that there is no need for change,
no need for conversion, that Christian moral ideals do not
present a challenge. Thinking this way might lead to self-
deception and to a neglect of the challenge and ideals that
Christian morality should present. It could also lead to
pride and to the illusion that living as a Christian is "pick-

---

[15] Francesca Ambrogetti and Sergio Rubin, *Pope Francis: His Life in His Own Words:
Conversations With Jorge Bergoglio* (New York: G.P. Putnam's Sons, 2010), pp. 41-42.

ing yourself up by your bootstraps" and becoming a "self-made Christian."

The other way is to see Christian morality and Christian living as an impossible task. Christian moral laws are looked upon as a terrible burden and the Christian life is basically inhuman and even, some might think, anti-human. Looking back on my life I suspect that through high school I leaned much more toward the second way of thinking than toward the first. Moral laws seemed arbitrary to me and embracing the Christian way of living seemed nearly impossible. When I reached graduate school I discovered that a number of the atheistic philosophers I studied thought of Christianity as basically anti-human. They were not only atheists but even anti-theists. They thought they had to kill the idea of God in order that human beings might be free to develop and grow into maturity, to develop their talents and to be true citizens of this world.

I think that each person trying to be a Christian has to be ready to change and grow. My vision of the Christian life is that each person is called to an ongoing process of conversion and growth. Each person is on an adventurous journey with Christ and the journey won't end in this world. But this journey is not one in which we should lose our humanity. The reverse is true. God's plan for us is to help us become more human, to reach a new and wonderful depth in our humanity. Christian morality is not against what is human but rather it is a guide to becoming our best selves.

We want to understand reality and grasp truth as deeply as we can. For many of us this involves putting on the mind of Christ. We want our consciousness to be

Christ-centered, formed, shaped, and illuminated by our faith in Christ. I find it very helpful to read great writers and their writings help me to see more deeply into the mystery of God and into what it means to be human. Of course there is no book that is the equal of sacred scripture. God's Word has a special power to enlighten us. We want not only to think differently but to live differently. The move from selfishness to unselfishness, from self-centeredness to concern about others is a lifelong task but it is to this that we are called. I imagine that each person's love affair with God is unique to that person but I think that one way to fall more in love with God is by responding through prayer to God's loving presence. I am thinking of both liturgical prayer, especially the Eucharist, and of private prayer. If we take God seriously then we should take our prayer life seriously. Our ongoing conversion should not be dreaded or feared but rather welcomed as an invitation from God Who loves us beyond our capacity to imagine.

Growth Through Self-revelation

For many years I thought of friendships, and indeed all interpersonal relationships among human beings, as more or less extrinsic to religion and to spiritual growth. Though I never thought of friendships as sinful or somehow harmful, I did not think of them as central to taking the Christian life seriously. There was a time when I thought of friendships as something of a distraction, certainly not as essential to religion. Now I believe intimate friendships are very much connected to our relationship to God. One of life's great gifts, friendship can be one of the most important ways through which God communicates with us. Examining the ways that we interact with our friends might give us some idea of how we interact with God. In his book, *The Jesuit Guide to (Almost) Everything: A Spirituality for Real Life*, Father James Martin, S.J., writes the following:

> *"Friendship is a blessing in any life. For believers it is also one of the ways God communicates God's own friendship. But for friendship to flourish, neither the friendship nor the friend can be seen as an object to be possessed. One of the best gifts to give a friend is freedom."* [16]

My thinking about friendships has been greatly influenced by my friends, who have been marvelous blessings, graces, and gifts in my life. Concerning my friends I often ask myself "What did I do to deserve such friends?" Of course the answer is that I did not do anything. My friends and all friends are gifts. We can act in such a way that our friendships deepen, but basic to every friendship is a gift that is not forced or compelled or the product of manipulation. It is true that at the human level friends are self-gifts but a more profound truly amazing self-gift is offered to us by God through inviting us into relationship. No matter how often we reflect on this or how deep our appreciation of this is, I think it should always appear awesome to us that God, the Creator of the entire universe, has reached out to us in love.

In his *Person and Being*, Father W. Norris Clarke, S.J., emphasizes that it is essential to our personal growth that we reveal ourselves to others. Our actions reveal who we

---

[16] James Martin, *The Jesuit Guide to Almost Everything: A Spirituality for Real Life* (HarperOne, An Imprint of HarperCollins, 2010), p. 243.

are. By acting we "speak ourselves." I often tell the college students I teach that I cannot really hide from them. The way I dress, the way I walk, my manner of speaking, my excitement and enthusiasm or my lack of excitement and enthusiasm, all these reveal me. While I may successfully not reveal the depth of my self, I think that the students will know that I am trying to conceal myself, that I am not whom I appear to be.

Father Clarke writes the following:

> *"It is connatural for us, giving full expression to the dynamism of existence flowing through us at its most intense as personalized, to reveal, manifest, express ourselves to other persons, to make manifest who we are, what we believe in, stand for etc., in a word, our story. Only when we express ourselves to others—including God, of course, who is infinitely self-expressive in his Word, the Son, and the Holy Spirit—can we come to know our own selves fully. As we mentioned earlier in speaking of self-possession, we do not start off in luminous self-understanding but must go out to the world and other persons first, then return to know ourselves by reflecting on our actions, whether and how they express who and what we really are or would like to be."* [17]

How much I come to know myself depends to some extent on how much I allow others to know me. This insight of Father Clarke's fascinates me. If I am going to conceal myself from others then I will not come to know myself as deeply as I would if I allowed others to know

---

[17] W. Norris Clarke, *Person and Being* (Milwaukee: Marquette University Press, 1993), p. 91.

me deeply. In God's providential plan we really are tied together. One way of expressing this truth is "I cannot know myself as deeply as possible without you and you cannot know yourself as deeply as possible without me." How we relate to others is extremely important.

Father Clarke argues that a person should be totally open and honest at least with one other person. Of course it is important that we be completely honest with God, but I agree with Father Clarke that for personal development it is very valuable to be able to reveal the deepest level of personality to another human person. I hope that this could happen between spouses, best friends, or with a spiritual director. Perhaps it is not as necessary concerning negative aspects of our personalities as it is concerning what might be called the positive riches of our personalities. I am not imagining bragging or boasting but rather sharing what we take to be our most cherished, most intimate and deepest dreams, desires, and hopes. Sharing these with another may be one way of preserving them and might eventually lead to acting on them so that they leave the world of dreams and become incarnated in reality.

Giftedness of God

Several years ago I found that I was focusing on one word to sum up everything important that I believed about God and myself. In fact the word captured for me whatever vision I had of all of reality. The word was a kind of shorthand way of expressing my faith. How this came about I am not certain but I know that I used the word when I was doing centering prayer and also when I was trying to write something about people's relationship with God. It even influenced how I structured my homilies and how I emphasized what I thought both the congregation and I should focus on in our efforts at imitating Jesus. The word was "Eucharist." The doctrine of the Eucharist seems to sum up for me everything that we believe as Catholics.

Many years ago when I was working in a parish I discovered that about twenty-five percent of the Catholics who lived in the parish did not attend Sunday Mass regularly. Often I would say of them "They have the faith, they just don't practice it." Today I would not describe people who do not attend Sunday Mass regularly as "having the faith." I don't know who has the faith. But my understanding of the Eucharist is that it is so central to the meaning of being a Catholic that if someone does not attend the Eucharist regularly I don't know what it would mean to describe that person as Catholic. Is being Catholic the same as having a particular nationality? Is being Catholic only something cultural?

A priest friend of mine told me about a conversation he had with a man who insisted that he was Catholic though he did not believe in the Incarnation. The man defended his claim to being Catholic by citing how he enjoyed Church architecture, music, and religious art. With little if any success, my friend tried to explain that there are some doctrines that are central to the Catholic faith. One of those doctrines is the Incarnation, the truth that the Son of God took on a human nature while remaining divine. The Eucharist is another central doctrine of Catholicism. I don't know what it would mean to state that a person who did not believe in the real presence of the Risen Christ in the Eucharist was a Catholic or had the faith.

In recent years, and I am not certain how this has happened, the word Eucharist as my "summary word" to express what I believe about God and the human race and indeed to express the meaning of all of reality, has given way to the word "gift." In relation to us, God is giver; in relation to God, we are gifted, that is receivers of gifts. All of created reality is God's gift to us. Of course God's greatest gift is God's Son. This vision of reality is present in what I have identified as my favorite poem, #34, by the Jesuit priest Gerard Manley Hopkins. After stating that each being speaks itself. Hopkins turns toward the person in grace, the person who has accepted God's self-gift:

> *"I say more: the just man justices;*
> *Keeps grace: that keeps all his goings graces;*
> *Acts in God's eye what in God's eye he is-*
> *Christ—for Christ plays in ten thousand places,*
> *Lovely in limbs, and lovely in eyes not his*
> *To the Father through the features of men's faces."* [18]

Hopkins' poem expresses with great beauty and marvelous language what I mean to express when I use the word gift to express what is most important about all of created reality. The Father sees us as the Body of Christ.

The Mystery and Poverty of Finite Being

Thinking about the mystery of being I am smiling because I am recalling a retreat experience of mine when I was a student in the major seminary. Back in those days the seminary retreats were completely silent. Around the time of the retreat I was reading a book by the great French Catholic philosopher Jacques Maritain. It may have

---

[18] Hopkins, *op. cit.*

been his *A Preface to Metaphysics.* In the book Maritain was suggesting ways that a person might become aware of the mystery of being, the mystery of existence. One of Maritain's suggestions was that a person should take a blade of grass into his or her hand and just zero in on the existence or being of the blade. The point of the exercise, I imagine, was to help a person get a sense of what it means to be. It was an attempt at grasping to some extent the marvel of existing. I can recall sitting on a bench in this huge field with a blade of grass in the palm of my hand trying to come to understand the mystery of being. If anyone was watching me, I must have been quite a sight!

The Catholic personalist existentialist Gabriel Marcel wrote a two-volume work entitled *The Mystery of Being.* My understanding of Marcel's philosophical vision is that being is the realm of value, the realm of the transcendent, the dimension of reality that is most important. Marcel suggested that there are some significant acts that can lead us into the mystery of being, that can put us in touch with what really matters. For Marcel faith, fidelity, hope, and love were such acts. These significant human acts can lead us into the mystery of being, into what is most important in life. Marcel contrasts having with being. Having suggests possession and control, perhaps even manipulation, being invites surrender. Marcel makes much of what he calls in French *disponibilite.* I think the best translation for that term is "available." The person who is available is ready to give himself away. He or she is ready to serve, to put love into action.

What does all this have to do with Maritain's blade of grass? I think what links Maritain's suggestion to Marcel's insights into the mystery of being is the total gratuity of creation. God did not have to create. Every being, and I mean *every* being, is a free gift from God. Marcel believed that the free love that God bestows in creating can be experienced by us through acts of faith, fidelity, hope, and love. When we make ourselves available to serve and to help others, we are imitating the graciousness and love that God gives freely. In the seminary during that retreat, what I was trying to do at the suggestion of Maritain, was experience the gift of existence bestowed by God on that blade of grass. The poverty of the blades of grass made them totally dependent on God. A question that many philosophers pose to their students is "Why is there something rather than nothing?" I suppose all sorts of responses might be given by students ranging from "How should I know?" to "Because of the Big Bang and evolution" but the answer that we can offer from our faith is because of love. When some of the greatest minds in the history of thought have asked why God created the best answer they could come up with was that this is what love does, love gives, love desires to share.

The mystery of being points us beyond life on earth. Seymour Cain in his book *Gabriel Marcel* comments on Marcel's view of immortality. Cain writes the following:

> *"Death for other men and for their good, for instance, is always death before the transcendent Other—even when it is an 'atheist humanist' who sacrifices his life. Absolute fidelity to a being transcends and conquers death. 'To love a being is to say thou wilt never die',* . . . *Anything else is betrayal—it is to give up one's beloved to death and take silence and invisibility for annihilation. For absolute fidelity, rooted in transcendence, the beloved dead is not an image*

or a memory or a shadow, but the 'still existing' *for me of what* 'no longer exists', *a permanent, unfailing presence, with which I am in real relation."* [19]

I agree completely with Marcel's view of fidelity, faith, hope, and love as ways of entering into the mystery of being. In spite of what physicians or undertakers might tell us about the beloved who has died, love tells us that the beloved is alive beyond the grave. The beloved is a gift for eternity. Pope Francis' comments on death echo Marcel's insights. The Holy Father said:

"When I say, 'I believe that there is a hereafter,' in reality I am saying that I am sure of it. *In theological language, to believe is a certainty, and eternal life takes shape here; in the experience of the encounter with God, it begins in the amazement of the encounter."* [20]

Referring to scenes in the Bible, Pope Francis comments:

"Seeing God is not understood as a punishment, but rather it is the experience of entering into another dimension and knowing that one is headed there. This is the richest interpretation that I find in the Bible with regard to the afterlife. You cannot live in a state of awe permanently, but the memory of that moment is never forgotten. We believe that there is another life because we have already begun to feel it here. It is not a mellow feeling, but rather something astonishing through which God has revealed Himself to us." [21]

---

[19] Seymour Cain, *Gabriel Marcel* (South Bend, Indiana: Regnery/Gateway, Inc., 1961), p. 86.

[20] Bergoglio and Skorka, *op. cit.*, pp. 85-86.

[21] *Ibid.*, p. 84.

CHAPTER TWO

Poverty of Spirit: Joy, Hope, and Love

ONE way to ruin a friendship is by being too posses-sive. We can be tempted to want our friends to fulfill all our needs. And when they don't, we blame them. No finite being, no creature is going to be able to fulfill all our needs and to expect them to is to impose an impossible burden on them. Marriage counselors tell me that often when a couple comes for counseling either the wife or husband starts the session by proclaiming that the other partner does not completely fulfill him or her. If someone said that to me, I would be tempted to say, "So you did not marry God? You married a flawed, finite human being, something like yourself!"

Christian Joy

Sometimes preparing a talk is an important learning experience for the speaker. I thought I knew what Chris-tian joy was until I had to give a lecture about it and then I found that it was easier to say what it was *not* than to say what it was. There is a statement from Abbot Dom Marmion that has appeared on numerous holy cards: "Joy is the echo of God's life in us." Often I have quoted the statement in homilies. Now that I had to give a talk about joy, I was forced to ask myself just what Dom Marmion meant.

Joy is not the same as giddiness. A person who has Christian joy does not have to walk around grinning. Apparently I do this on the campus of St. John's University. Recently another professor, seeing me approach, said "Here comes the smiling priest!" Often I'm not even aware that I'm smiling. I'm not sure whether my lack of awareness is a good or a bad personality trait. But Christian joy is not necessarily evidenced through smiling. In fact someone might have Christian joy and yet at some moment or moments be unable to smile.

Christian joy, I have come to believe, is something deeply religious, perhaps even mystical. This special kind of joy comes from a deep awareness of God's love and of the Spirit's presence within us. It is necessary for me to remind myself occasionally that the Holy Spirit's presence is not an event that happens only in dramatic situations or only when a sacred rite such as the Eucharist is being celebrated. The Holy Spirit's presence is a constant and the Holy Spirit is not merely an interested observer. The Holy Spirit, the Spirit of Love, is actively present, inviting, encouraging, inspiring. As I thought about Christian joy I had a strange experience: I simultaneously experienced insight and darkness. The experience was a chiaroscuro of light and darkness. I turned to that marvelous source for information about anything to do with the Catholic understanding of holiness: *The New Dictionary of Catholic Spirituality*. There I found the following:

> *"Far more than a feeling state or a mere heightened sense of pleasure, joy in the Christian life refers to a*

basic disposition and a fundamental attunement to the self-giving of God in Christ. To rejoice in the midst of suffering puts a strain on our ordinary conception of joy and enjoyment. This is because the joy of which Scripture and the tradition speak takes a peculiar object—the revelation of God in Christ. Thus Mary's Magnificat rejoices in 'God my Savior.'

". . . Joy is thus ingredient in the very pattern of life constituted by trust in God, in, with, and through Jesus Christ. Every activity and relationship in service of God and neighbor shares in a joyful quality. Serving the neighbor becomes an 'enjoyment,' one of the chief ends of human existence. Such joy is not contingent upon fortune, good or bad, but is grounded in faith that God is Creator and Redeemer of the world.

". . . In sum, joy occupies a central place among the Christian affections, yet it is also characteristic of all activities begun and completed in faith." [22]

Commenting on Christian joy, Pope Francis said:

"Christian life is bearing witness with cheerfulness, as Jesus did. Saint Thérèse of Lisieux said that a sad saint is a holy sadness." [23]

Christian joy comes from a deep awareness of God's love for us. We do not believe in Christ's teachings because they are interesting or provocative ideas. We believe in Christ's teachings because we believe in Christ, because we have made a commitment to the Lord. What can we do to foster Christian joy in our lives? Some silent

[22] Don E. Saliers, "Joy" in *The New Dictionary of Catholic Spirituality* (Editor Michael Donney, A Michael Glazier Book, The Liturgical Press, Collegeville, Minnesota, 1993), pp. 577-578.
[23] Ambrogetti and Rubin, op. cit., pp. 27-28.

time each day with God can help—time in which we do not speak to God but rather listen to what God is saying to us. We may hear God saying "I love you." I believe that if we spend silent time with God our awareness of God's love for us will increase and deepen. Reflecting on self as gifted by God can also deepen Christian joy. Each Christian's journey should be joyful. In every story, God's gifts abound. At the deepest level our life in the world should be characterized by a profound joy. Father Norris Clarke, S. J. has some marvelous insights into the relationship between a person and others. Clarke sees the human journey as a developing presence between the person and the world, more specifically between a person's presence to self and a person's presence to other. He writes the following:

> *"Thus the life of every human person unfolds as a journey of the spirit through an ever developing spiral circulation between self-presence and active self-expressive presence to others, between the "I" and the world, both personal and sub-personal, between inward-facing self-possession and outward-facing openness to the other. And, paradoxically, the more intensely I am present to myself at one pole, the more intensely I am present and open to others at the other. And reciprocally, the more I make myself truly present to the others as an "I" or self, the more I must also be present to myself, in order that it may be truly I that is present to them, and not a mask."* [24]

Clarke has articulated a profound truth about human persons. How I am present to myself can greatly influence

---

[24] Clarke, *op. cit.*, pp. 69-70.

how I am present to other persons, and how I am present to other persons can greatly influence how I am present to myself. One of the ways that we grow as persons is through our relationships with other persons. Unfortunately one of the ways that we fail to grow is through poor relationships with other persons.

I am thinking of two people I knew when I was doing graduate work in philosophy many years ago. One person once told me that everyone was his friend. I thought that was amazing, that he could be so open to so many people. When I would walk around the campus with him he would greet many people with comments such as "How are your courses going?" or "How are your parents doing?" Initially I was very impressed that someone could be so welcoming and receptive to other persons. However as I came to know him better, it seemed to me that he had no close friends. He had many acquaintances but did not seem to have any deep relationships. He was quite guarded and would not allow anyone to get very close. The other person was a professor who may have been the most free person I have ever met. He was extremely busy, teaching, writing, giving extra lectures outside the university and yet when he was with someone, for example a student, he was completely present, as though he had nothing else to do that day but be present to the student. I think that physically he was blessed with great stamina but more importantly he was a mature, composed, exceptionally intelligent person who had decided to give his life in service to others. Seeing deeply into ourselves, realizing that we are gifted by God, can nourish Christian joy.

Hope: The Earthly Virtue

The expression "the earthly virtue" seems to me to fit the virtue of hope. This is probably due to the way that I think about the virtue as having one foot in the next world and one foot in this. Hope is focused on the next life with the Risen Lord but it is also crucially important for us as we try to direct our lives in this world. St. Paul was of course completely correct in claiming that love is the greatest virtue and as I have grown older that has become more and more obvious to me, but I think that hope must be right below it in terms of importance in our efforts at living as followers of Christ. I agree with the statement of St. John of the Cross that in the evening of our lives we will be judged by how we have loved but I also think that how we love is related to how deeply we hope.

I have been trying to be more hopeful, more trusting in God's love, for more than 60 years. When I was studying in the seminary to become a priest, for one entire year, at the advice of a spiritual director, I read everything that I could get my hands on about the virtue of hope. I read books, pamphlets, and essays. The plan was to fill my consciousness with the importance of trusting in God. A few years ago I came upon a quote from the theologian Gordon Kaufman. It is about the mystery of God's Providence. The quote spoke to me and still does. When I have shared it with others it seems to have helped them as well. It presents a beautiful view of reality and of the decisions and choices that people make. What is most important about Kaufman's statement is that it is true. He wrote the following:

"If man could believe that the historical context into which he has been thrown were meaningful, if he could believe it to be the loving personal decision and purpose of a compassionate Father Who is moving all history toward a significant goal, then anxiety would be dissolved. If he could believe his existence and decisions and actions had an indispensable place within larger purposes shaping the overall movement of history, and that even his stupid blunders and willful perversities could be rectified and redeemed, his anxiousness and guilt could give place to confidence, creativeness and hope." [25]

Pope Francis, stressing the importance of hope, said the following:

"We have to take on the responsibility of our journey; in it will appear all of our creativity, and our work to transform this world, but we must not forget that we are on a path toward a promise. To journey is the creative responsibility to fulfill the command of God: to grow, be fruitful and subdue the earth. The first Christians were united around the image of death with hope, and they used as a symbol the anchor. So, hope was the anchor that one had dug into the shore, and they held on to the rope in order to advance without losing their way. Salvation is in hope, that it will be fully revealed to us, but in the meantime we are holding on to the rope and doing what we believe that we have to do. Saint Paul tells us: 'In hope we are saved.' " [26]

---

[25] Gordon Kaufman
[26] Bergoglio and Skorka, *op. cit.*, p. 87.

Imagining God

Though there were times in my life when I thought of God as a bystander, picturing God as observing me but not actively involved in my choices, this is not the God whom Jesus revealed. God is constantly active in our lives, loving us, inviting us, inspiring us. If God is pure self-gift, and this is the least inaccurate image we can have of God, then God is in a dynamic relation with us at every moment of our lives. We are called to surrender to God. Of course if we are conscious at the moment of our death, the most important act that we can perform is to surrender to God Who loves us more than we can imagine. But it is not just at the moment of death that we are called to surrender. We do not redeem or save ourselves. God offers us salvation and redemption but we must choose to accept God's gift. St. Augustine said that though God created us without our consent, God will not save us without our consent. There are many realities in our experience that can frighten us, even frighten us so much that we are afraid to act. That is where hope comes into play. Hope reminds us to trust in God's love for us and that the victory has been won for us by Jesus' death and resurrection. Hope does not mean that everything will turn out the way that we want. It does mean that at the end even our best wishes and dreams will be exceeded by what God has planned for us. Everyone's life is a great drama, an adventure in grace, a journey toward the goal that Jesus has won for us. On that journey we are never alone. Hope reminds us of this profound truth and encourages us to live in the light of that truth.

By chance (or was it providence?) I came upon a small book *Poverty of Spirit* by Joannes Metz. At one time a disciple of the great German theologian Karl Rahner, Metz eventually moved away from Rahner's theology and constructed his own theological vision. I suspect that he thought Rahner's theology dealt too much with the individual and did not focus sufficiently on community and social problems. *Poverty of Spirit* is a gem. Within its pages are wonderful philosophical and theological insights into the mystery of the human person and the mystery of God. My guess is that one reason that I enjoyed reading Metz's book so much is that the philosophy that the German thinker uses is very similar to the philosophy I teach college students. Metz's insights fit perfectly into Pope Francis' spirituality of poverty. At the beginning of his foreword, Metz writes:

> *"Becoming a human being involves more than conception and birth. It is a mandate and a mission, a command and a decision. We each have an open-ended relationship to ourselves. We do not possess our being unchallenged; we cannot take our being for granted as God does. . . . Other animals, for example, survive in mute innocence and cramped necessity. With no future horizons, they are what they are from the start; the law of their life and being is spelled out for them, and they resign themselves to these limits without question. . . . We, however, are challenged and questioned from the depths of our boundless spirit. Being is entrusted to us as a summons, which we are each to accept and consciously acknowledge. . . . To become human through the exercise of our freedom—that is the law of our Being."* [27]

---

[27] Metz, *Poverty of Spirit* (Translated by John Drury. Inclusive language version by Carole Farris, New York: Paulist Press, 1968), p. 3.

After I read the first sentences of the foreword, I was hooked. Metz expresses succinctly, yet powerfully, what I consider some of the most important truths about the human person, truths I teach, write about, discuss and try to live. That being human is both a mandate and a mission, a command and a decision, I find provocative, exciting, challenging, and inspiring. By creating us as conscious free persons, God has built into our nature a call. We are not finished and God is not finished with us. Our lives are adventures in grace, adventures in trying to be less self-centered and selfish and more unselfish and loving. We are creatures summoned by God, called by God to live our lives as gifts, gifts to God and to others. This is the ultimate meaning of being human. There is a purpose and a goal and a direction built into our nature as persons. We are magnetized by God but we are free. We can turn away from the mandate and the mission. We are the only creatures in our experience who are free. This is a tremendous blessing but it also involves risk. How we direct our freedom will decide the type of persons we become. God is creating us from nothing but because of our freedom we can influence our destiny. Recognition of our dependence on God can help us cultivate poverty of spirit and also make us more aware of our freedom.

The view of God that anti-theists attack was on my mind as I read *Poverty of Spirit* because the German theologian presents a view of God that stresses that God is all for us, that not only is God not an enemy but rather God's presence in our lives frees us and enables us to grow and develop beyond our plans and wildest dreams. Metz writes the following:

"God does not undermine our humanity, but protects and insures it. God's truth makes us free (cf. Jn 8:32). Unlike the pagan gods, God does not expropriate our humanity. In drawing us to the Divine self, God sets us free. God is the guardian of our humanity, who lets us be what we are. When God draws the creature near, the creature becomes all the more important. When God draws near, the glow of our humanity shines even more brightly before us. God brightens our true greatness as human beings. . . .

"God has come to us in grace. We have been endowed with God's life and our life made God's. . . . God's grace does not cause estrangement and excess, as sin does. It reveals the full depths of our destiny (resulting from God's salvific initiative in history), which we could not have imagined by ourselves." [28]

How we think of God greatly influences how we think of ourselves and how we think of ourselves greatly influences how we think of God. Each of us has an image of self and each of us has an image of God. To the extent that we allow those images to influence us, they will play a very significant role in our experiences and in our relationships with others. I knew a young man who had a terrible self-image. He was intelligent, witty, good-looking and a genuinely good person. I once asked him to tell me one good thing about himself. He could not mention even one. I could have mentioned twenty. How did he get that self-image? Who gave it to him? I don't know but because of it he had trouble with all his relationships. Because he could not love himself, he could not love anyone.

---

[28] *Ibid*, pp. 20-21.

It seems paradoxical to me that poverty of spirit reveals our greatness. Poverty of spirit might lead some to think that we are less than nothing, that we have no intrinsic value, that our dependence on God reveals our basic worthlessness. The opposite is true. God helps us be what we are. God's presence in our lives does not erase or annihilate us. Rather God's presence in our lives allows us to grow as persons. Our poverty of spirit, strange as this may seem to us, allows us to appreciate what an almighty loving God has done and is doing for us. Once we recognize our neediness, which is another way of identifying what we have been calling our poverty of spirit, we can become aware that we are made by God for God. Our consciousness, which is created by God, is directed toward God, our will which is created by God, is only going to find fulfillment in a loving relationship with God. No finite being will ever satisfy us or fulfill us. To be human is to be magnetized by God. The deepest level of ourselves is oriented toward God and nothing less than God will satisfy us. Poverty of spirit tells us who we are and it calls our attention to Who God is. I love the expression "the theatre of God's grace." What it signifies is that God is actively and lovingly present in every person's life, not only in the Christian's life but in the lives of atheists and agnostics. Every person's life is an adventure in grace, a drama that involves the person but also God. Each of us lives in the theatre of God's grace. How each of us responds to God's loving presence in our lives leads either to our salvation or to our loss of a love relationship with God. Occasionally I have encountered Catholics who are upset when they hear that God is lovingly present in the life of every person. This somehow seems to offend their sense of justice. They may feel that Catholics deserve God's love in some way that others do not deserve it. It is almost suggesting that we are the "good guys" and all others are the "bad guys."

It is crucially important that all of us remind ourselves that God's love for us is pure gift. God does not love us because we are lovable, but rather we are lovable because God loves us and we should rejoice that this love extends to everyone. A human person not loved by God is a fiction. People may be touched by God's grace without even knowing it. For us to be influenced by God's grace it is not necessary that we be aware that we are responding to God's loving presence. We may not be explicitly thinking of God when we perform some good action. Whenever there is a genuinely good act, whenever there is an unselfish action, that action is done because of the presence of the Holy Spirit even if the person who does the action does not think of the Holy Spirit while doing the action.

Before the presence of the transcendent God, we can become very aware of just how impoverished our being is. Our poverty is, as it were, underlined in light of God's greatness. We can seem to be nothing and of no value before the Infinite. Yet it is precisely God's loving presence that calls attention to our importance, our significance, our dignity and our destiny. God's love creates us and redeems us. We are who we are only because of God's creative loving presence. We are tied to God. That we are tied to God reveals our identity and our vocation. We are called by God into a future of growth and development. Metz says that we have an "insatiable interest in the Absolute." Our minds and wills are oriented toward God.

No truth less than God will ever fulfill our desire to know and no good except the Infinite Good, which is God, will ever fulfill our desire to love. When we focus our consciousness on God and direct our wills toward God we are not approaching either intellectually or volitionally some external object. God and we are inextricably joined. God is not finished with us after we are created by God. Built into the nature of the human person is a dynamism, a direction, if you like, a call to become more than we are. What seems like an impossible task becomes possible because of Christ's identification with us. Because of the Risen Christ's dwelling within us, because we share in God's own life, we become capable of doing what we could never do on our own. We have been bought at a great price, the death and resurrection of the Son of God, and that price has transformed our poverty into a graced richness. We have become a new creation. Commenting on the value and power of poverty when the church needs reform, Pope Francis said:

> *"All of a sudden figures like Mother Teresa of Calcutta appeared, and they stirred up the concept of the dignity of the human person, figures who wasted their time—because in some way the time was lost—in helping people die. These actions generate mystique and rejuvenate religious fervor. In the history of the Catholic Church the true reformers are the saints. They are the true reformers, those that change, transform, carry forward and resurrect the spiritual path. In another case, Francis of Assisi contributed an entire concept about poverty to Christianity in the face of the wealth, pride and vanity of the civil and ecclesial pow-*

ers of the time. He carried out a mysticism of poverty,
of dispossession and he has changed history." [29]

A GIFT-GIVING STORY

Everyone loves a story. Catholicism is a religion of stories. One of the great blessings to being a Catholic is that you should have a sense that you are part of a great story, that your individual story takes its ultimate meaning and significance from a bigger, larger, and all-encompassing story that gives your individual story its most important meaning. Today when people claim that they are adrift or that they can make no sense of what it means to be human, they are often claiming that they have been unable to find a meaningful, important story within which their own story fits and takes on significance. Many of the twentieth century's most gifted artists seem to have been in that predicament. Some were Catholics who when they lost their Catholic faith spent the rest of their lives looking for a substitute.

There are several reasons why I love Holy Week. One of the reasons is that during this wonder-filled week we review liturgically the entire history of salvation, God's story and our story. The week is about God's involvement with people and that includes us. The story of the Old Testament is reviewed, the story of the New Testament is reviewed, and that means that our story is reviewed. That we do this liturgically makes the entire experience much more than a history lesson or a merely academic exercise. To review the history of salvation liturgically means that we are praying with the Risen Lord. The liturgy is much

---

[29] Bergoglio and Skorka, *op. cit.*, p. 231.

more than my private prayer, even much more than a group of friends praying together. The liturgy is Christ praying and we are in union with Him, offering Him and ourselves to the Father. Liturgical prayer takes its great value and importance not primarily from us but from Christ. The liturgy is Christ's prayer to the Father.

The word that sums up the entire Holy Week liturgy for me is the word "gift." Our relationship with God is founded on gift, and the gift is God Himself. The entire history of salvation can be looked at as an ongoing dialogue between God and people, God giving and human persons receiving. That dialogue continues today. It is celebrated at every Eucharist but the celebrations during Holy Week are special.

Parts of the Holy Week liturgy seem especially powerful. The reading of the Lord's Passion both on Palm Sunday and on Good Friday are very powerful moments. The prayers for just about every intention after the reading of the Passion on Good Friday I also find powerful. It is as though the Church, having recalled Jesus' death, has a new confidence in the power of that death to touch everyone. Imitating her Head, who stretched his arms out in love to include every member of the human race, the Church excludes no one as she prays. The first words of the magnificent hymn the Exultet sung at the Saturday Vigil should fill all our hearts with joy:

> *"Rejoice heavenly powers! Sing, choirs of angels!*
> *Exult, all creation around God's throne!*
> *Jesus Christ, our King, is risen!*
> *Sound the trumpet of salvation!*
> *Rejoice, O earth, in shining splendor,*

radiant in the brightness of Your King!
Christ has conquered! Glory fills you!"

Theologian Richard Viladesau has written the following about the Resurrection:

> *"Of course the message of the resurrection speaks of what is 'ahead' and 'above': it looks forward, beyond death, to new and transcendent life with God.. But it also looks 'backward' and 'within' to the heart of earthly life—that of Jesus, and our own.*
>
> *"The resurrection of Jesus means that it was precisely the one that was crucified who is now in glory. Therefore the resurrection first of all validates Jesus' way of living in the world. It proclaims that he was right in his message and his conduct: right in his message of service and forgiveness, and in seeing God's love and affirmation as present and triumphant, right in placing love as a value above all others; right not to grasp at life, but to give himself over in trust even in death.*
>
> *"It means furthermore that our lives are validated insofar as we live by the same convictions and relationships that animated Jesus."* [30]

God speaks to human beings. I don't mean that we hear a voice. Perhaps the saints occasionally have the experience of hearing a "divine voice," but I don't think most of us have that experience. God speaks to us in a uniquely divine way. That God's way of communicating with us is different from the way that other humans communicate with us does not mean that God's way is inferi-

---

[30] Viladesau, *The Word In and Out of Season: Homilies for the Major Feasts, Christmas, Easter, Weddings, and Funerals* (New York: Paulist Press, 2001), pp. 50-51.

or or less real. In fact, God's way, though mysterious, is more real. God might speak to us through our consciences, through nature, through historical events, through art, through our families and friends. When God speaks to us, God calls. God's speech is never idle or superficial or without a purpose or a plan. God's speech is for the sake of relationship. God's speech, God's call, is an invitation, a unique invitation that only God can offer.

When God speaks, calls, and invites, God supports. This is important to remember. God will never call us to the impossible, never call us to do that which we cannot do, to accomplish what we cannot accomplish. Whatever God is calling us to or inviting us into, God will be constantly present supporting us. We are never alone. God will never abandon us.

For a considerable time in my life I resisted listening to God because I was afraid. I believed that if we surrendered to God's will, we would be saints but without fully realizing what I was doing, I resisted God's presence, resisted surrendering. This was really foolish on my part. God wants what is good for us more than we want what is good for us.

Resurrection: Poverty Redeemed

Memory plays tricks on us but I am fairly certain that my recollection of studying the Resurrection of Christ when I was a seminarian is accurate. At that time, over 50 years ago, we studied dogmatic theology from a manual, a kind of textbook. A great deal of what we studied in theology back then is now out of date but even then I was surprised at how little time and reading we devoted to Jesus' Resurrection. The lack of emphasis on the Resurrection when I studied theology seems incredible. Now all Christian theology is centered on the Resurrection. Not only is the entire New Testament now studied in light of the Resurrection but also the Old Testament. Many things happened to bring about the change. One of the most influential events was the publication of *The Resurrection: A Biblical Study* by F.X. Durrwell, C.SS.R.

It is probably impossible to overemphasize the impact that Father Durrwell's book had. It is an excellent example to indicate that theology is historical: new insights are reached, new emphases happen, and theology changes. Of course Catholic theology should never change in such a way that it contradicts Revelation or the Church's infallible teaching. In the foreword to his book, Father Durrwell notes that some theologians studied redemption without mentioning the Resurrection, that Christ's work of redemption was looked at as consisting in His incarnation, His life, and His death on the cross. After lamenting the neglect of the Resurrection in the study of redemption and its absence in the thought of many theologians and identifying it as one of the inexhaustible mysteries of our salvation, Father Durrwell writes the following:

> *"When the Resurrection was mentioned, it was not so much to give it any part in our salvation as to show it as Christ's personal triumph over his enemies, and a kind of glorious counterblast to the years of humiliation he had endured to redeem us. In short, Christ's Resurrection was shorn of the tremendous significance seen in it by the first Christian teachers, and relegated to the background of the redemptive scheme. Such blindness naturally impoverished the whole theology of the Atonement.*

"Yet all that was needed was to listen to St. Paul, who says categorically: 'And if Christ be not risen again, your faith is vain, for you are yet in your sins (1 Cor 15:17).' 'Christ died for all . . . died for them and rose again (2 Cor 5:15).' 'Who was delivered up for our sins, and rose again for our justification (Rom 4:25).'

"This book was born out of my excitement over these key texts of St. Paul, and a wish to share with others this tremendously helpful realization of the mystery of Easter." [31]

Though I am no historian, I think that around the time that dogmatic theology was changing, there was also a scriptural renewal, a liturgical renewal, and significant changes in the study and understanding of spirituality. All of these were influenced by a renewed interest and insight into Christ's Resurrection. Perhaps one word can sum up our reaction to the Resurrection: Alleluia!

The power of Jesus' Resurrection touches everyone. Karl Rahner claimed that future Christians would have to be mystics or they would not have any faith. I suspect Rahner's statement means that in an increasingly secular atmosphere people's faith will be grounded in a personal experience of faith, in an experience of Christ's Spirit operative in their lives. Being mystical means having an immediate encounter with God. People have to become aware of the in-depth dimension of their lives and realize what it means. Commenting on Rahner's view, Father Michael Paul Gallagher uses the expression "wired for God" to indicate God's presence in every person's life, even in the lives of those who have not yet come to real-

---

[31] Francis X. Durrwell, *The Resurrection: A Biblical Study* (Translated by Rosemary Sheed. New York: Sheed and Ward, 1960), p. XXIII.

ize that God is present.[32] Perhaps many of us are reluctant to think that we are being called to be mystics, indeed to be saints. It is amazing, but so is God's love for us.

Human Person as Openness to God

In the early 1960s my bishop at that time asked me to do graduate work in philosophy with the goal of obtaining a doctorate. The bishop was planning a four year college seminary, and he wanted me to get the doctorate so that I could teach at the college seminary. Though it had been nine years since I had studied philosophy in college, I knew that I wanted to write my doctoral dissertation on some aspect of the human person. If I had known about his philosophy at the time I was doing graduate work, I would have written on the Scottish philosopher, John Macmurray. Years later I became acquainted with Macmurray's thought and I was able to persuade three friends, who were doing graduate work, to write their dissertations on Macmurray. All three eventually received their doctoral degrees. Though I do not agree with all of Macmurray's ideas, I do find much of his philosophy interesting and even inspiring. His thought reminds me of the philosophy of Martin Buber.

In trying to wed the vision of St. Thomas Aquinas with contemporary existentialism, phenomenology, and personalism in his *Person and Being*, W. Norris Clarke, S.J., uses Macmurray's philosophy as an example of personalism. In discussing the relational aspect of the human person, Clarke, relying on Macmurray's insights, writes the following:

---

[32] Michael Paul Gallagher, *Faith Maps: Ten Religious Explorers from Newman to Joseph Ratzinger* (New York: Paulist Press, 2010), p. 43.

"Let us explore more in detail this relational aspect of the human person, beginning from the bottom up. The initial relationality of the human person towards the outer world of nature and other persons is primarily receptive, in need of actualizing its latent potentialities from without. The human person as child first goes out towards the world as poor, as appealingly but insistently needy. The primary response partner is the mother, who meets the growing person's needs ideally with caring love. First she responds to the physical and basic psychic needs, then slowly draws forth over the early years the active interpersonal response of the child as an I to herself as Thou, by her active relating to the child precisely as a loving I to a unique, special, and beloved Thou, not just as a useful or interesting object or thing, or another instance of human nature. John Macmurray has beautifully described the process of personalization, of drawing out of latent potentiality the self-conscious awareness and active-interpersonal response of the growing child-person, first by the mother or her surrogate, then by the father, the whole family, the neighborhood community, the school, etc." [33]

I find Clarke's description of the gradual opening of the child-person to his or her surroundings and then moving from things to the personal, as found in the child's world through the mother and father, beautiful. Anyone who would take Clarke's description seriously would realize what a tremendous responsibility parents have in relation to their child's experience of reality. But not just parents. All of us have a responsibility to help one another be

---

[33] Clarke, *op. cit.*, pp. 72-73.

receptive to reality, to help one another see that reality is gift, "charged with the grandeur of God"!

Clarke's insights remind me of my responsibility as a teacher of philosophy. Though I think philosophy has to take second place in importance after theology, I do believe deeply in the importance of philosophy. After many years of reading and teaching philosophy, I have come to see that it can provide profound insights into the mystery of person, into the mystery of self, into the mystery of neighbors, into the mystery of God. Though philosophy cannot give us the truths that have been made available through the revelation of Christ, it can greatly enrich our lives. My task, similar to the task of every teacher, is how to help students come to see this. How can I communicate the great insights of Plato, Aristotle, Aquinas, Soren Kierkegaard and Gabriel Marcel to eighteen and nineteen year old students?

But Clarke is not only pointing out that we relate on the level of knowledge. He is also stressing that we relate interpersonally to other persons on the level of affectivity. We do not only find ideas or truth interesting and attractive but we are drawn toward the good present to us as personal, perhaps first revealed to us through mother and father. We are receptive not just on the level of knowing but also on the level of being loved and this experience of being loved calls us to love in return. Our capacity to relate, itself a gift, is dynamic and should be deepening and widening, reaching beyond parents, toward school, community and, most importantly, toward God.

The Gift of Love

Of the many things that I like about the personalist-existentialist philosophy of Gabriel Marcel and there are many, is his insight that some actions can move us into the mystery of being. Marcel stresses that acts of faith, hope, and love can move us beyond the ordinary workaday world into the dimension of value and of significance and of mystery, which I think, as I've mentioned, is what he means by the mystery of being. Becoming aware of the mystery of being is to become aware of what really matters, of what is most important in life, of the dimension of reality that reveals that we are not alone, that we are surrounded by a love that conquers even death. There is a dramatic scene in one of Gabriel Marcel's plays, *The Broken World*. In it a woman lives a meaningless, superficial existence in what she perceives to be an empty world. She tries desperately to establish meaningful and solid relations. She remains attentive for some sign that in spite of evidence to the contrary, there is significant meaning, that there is a dimension of human living that is accessible and that she is missing. The following statement is made by the woman who experiences the world as broken:

> *"Don't you sometimes have the impression that we are living . . . if it can be called living . . . in a broken world? Yes, broken as a broken watch. The spring does not work any more. In appearance nothing has changed. Everything is in its proper place. But if one puts the watch to one's ear . . . one no longer hears anything. You understand, the world, what we call the*

*world, the world of men . . . formerly it must have had
a heart. But it's as if the heart has ceased to beat."* [34]

Commenting on this passage in his book *Gabriel Marcel*,
Seymour Cain writes the following:

> *"The 'broken world' is a world without unity or
> community: everyone goes on about his own affairs,
> without real communication, without real meeting.
> There are merely chance collisions. 'There is no longer
> a centre, no longer a life, anywhere,' says the despair-
> ing lady. But she keeps listening, listening 'into the
> void.' The possibility of salvation, of attaining the full-
> ness of reality, comes to her through a message of com-
> munion and sustaining presence from a beloved friend
> who has died, from one beyond life, and as the play
> ends she seeks to bring the light of this encounter into
> the common, daily life of herself and her husband."* [35]

Today almost everyone I know is under pressure and
lives at a terribly frantic pace. I include myself in this
group. I always seem to be racing somewhere or trying to
make some deadline, usually a deadline that I have some-
what arbitrarily made up putting myself under unneces-
sary pressure. I notice that at almost any moment of the
day I can announce what time it is without even looking
at my watch. "To stop and smell the roses" as the saying
goes, is not easy to do. We really have to work at giving
ourselves a break, at making time for what is most important, for what is most in tune with what human living ultimately means. Reflecting on the presence of God in our
lives has convinced me that all is gift. We don't create our-

---

[34] Quoted in Seymour Cain, *Gabriel Marcel, op. cit.*, p. 60.
[35] *Ibid.*, p. 61.

selves, we don't save ourselves, we don't redeem ourselves. Our lives are surrounded by the giftedness of God. If those truths don't help us to be less anxious, and more hopeful and hope-filled, and indeed more joyful then I don't know what will.

Love Unites and Distinguishes

In his book *Personalism*, Emmanuel Mounier, whose philosophical vision greatly influenced Catholic Worker's founder Dorothy Day, stresses that love is creative of distinction. Some poetry and love songs can give the impression that lovers lose their identities in one another. Statements such as "I lose myself in you" or "I love you so much that I have become you" are misleading. In a union of love, persons do not lose their identity but rather become more themselves or deepen their identity.

The experience of loving and being loved makes a person more himself or herself. As far as I can figure out this deepening rather than loss of identity only happens in a union of love. It does not happen in other unions. For example if I have a jar of water and a jar of wine, if I pour a large amount of water into the jar that contains the wine eventually the wine will be gone and all that will be left will be water. The wine will have been subsumed by the water. In loving and being loved the lover and beloved do not lose their identity in each other but rather each creates the other. Each reaches a deeper level of his or her personhood.

There is no surer way of growing as a person than being in a deep love relationship. Mounier writes *"Real love is creative of distinction; it is a gratitude and a will towards*

another because he is other than oneself." [36] What I am emphasizing is the "otherness" of the other. Imagine a couple on
their wedding day. Each is very much in love with the
other. Imagine that their love relationship deepened over
the next twenty-five years. On their twenty-fifth anniver-
sary if the couple has not changed, then something went
wrong. The change will not be that each has become the
other; the change will be that each has reached a new level
of personal freedom and autonomy. Each will have created the other.

I don't think that we can ever exaggerate the importance and the power of love. If someone were to ask me
what love could not accomplish, I would respond "I don't
know. Love is so powerful that it has conquered death. I
cannot say what love cannot accomplish. If love can con-
quer death, then maybe it can accomplish anything."

In praising the power of love, Mounier writes the following:

> *"The communion of love, liberating him who*
> *responds to it, also liberates and reassures him who*
> *offers it. Love is the surest certainty that man knows;*
> *the one irrefutable, existential cogito: I love, therefore I*
> *am; therefore being is, and life has value (is worth the*
> *pain of living). Love does not reassure me simply as a*
> *state of being in which I find myself, for it gives me to*
> *someone else. Sartre has spoken of the eye of another as*
> *something that transfixes one, that curdles the blood;*
> *and of the presence of someone else as a trespass upon*
> *one, a deprivation or a bondage. What we speak of here*
> *is no less disturbing; it shakes me out of my self-assur-*

---

[36] Emmanuel Mounier, *Personalism* (Notre Dame, University of Notre Dame Press, 1950), p. 23.

*ance, my habits, my egocentric torpor; communica-
tion, even when hostile, is the thing that most surely
reveals me to myself."* [37]

I don't believe that Mounier's statements are extreme
or exaggerations. Loving does reveal the lover to himself
or herself. The deepest meaning of being and certainly the
deepest meaning of human existence is revealed through
loving and being loved. Everyone is called to be a lover,
everyone is called to be a self-gift. No matter what a person's vocation is, to be a human person is to be called to
be a self-gift. I try to be a self-gift as a priest-professor,
someone else tries to be a self-gift as a married person or
a parent, someone else as a single person. Mounier is
pointing out that both the atheistic and theistic views of
reality are challenging: one challenges us to recognize
absurdity, the other challenges us to respond to an invitation to love. Life is either a terrible burden that ultimately
is unintelligible or it is a gift.

A Journey Toward God

Thinking about the new evangelization has moved me
to reflect on just what is meant by a conversion. Two
thinkers who have helped me reflect on the experience of
conversion are St. Augustine and the great 20th century
Jesuit theologian Bernard Lonergan. When I read what
Lonergan wrote about conversion and tried to come up
with examples of the types of conversion that Lonergan
identified, I found parts of St. Augustine's *Confessions*
helpful.

The Jesuit theologian distinguished three types of conversion: an intellectual conversion, a moral conversion,

---
[37] *Ibid.*

and a spiritual or religious conversion. An intellectual conversion takes place when a person radically changes his or her way of looking at reality. For example a person who is a Communist comes to believe in Christianity. In such a case the person has gone from not believing that there is a God to believing that not only is there a God but God has become human. In his *Confessions* Augustine reports that once his vision of reality was Manichean, a view of reality which taught that there was an evil principle equal to God. Eventually Augustine rejected the Manichean view and embraced Christian faith. That was an intellectual conversion. Augustine's view of reality had changed radically from believing that there was an evil power equal to God to believing that there was one God Who was supreme.

After he embraced the Christian view of reality, Augustine continued to sin seriously. Though he had changed his vision of reality, he had not changed the way he lived. Eventually he did change the way that he lived and followed the moral teaching of the Church. That change was a moral conversion: Augustine not only believed but changed his conduct.

The third conversion that Lonergan identified is sometimes called a religious conversion or a spiritual conversion. Lonergan described it as falling in love with God. When Augustine underwent this third conversion, he was on his way to becoming one of the great saints of the Church. Lonergan wrote the following about religious or spiritual conversion:

> *"Such transforming love has its occasions, its conditions, its causes. But once it comes and as long as it*

lasts, it takes over. One no longer is one's own. Moreover, in the measure that this transformation is effective, development comes not merely from below upwards but more fundamentally from above downwards. There has begun a life in which the heart has reasons which reason does not know. There has been opened up a new world in which the old adage, 'Nothing is loved unless it is first known,' yields to a new truth, 'Nothing is truly known unless it is first loved.' It is such transforming love that enables Paul to say: 'The life I now live is not my life, but the life which Christ lives in me' " (Gal 2:20). [38]

The more I think about the three types of conversion, the more questions I have. Can someone have an intellectual conversion and not have it accompanied by a moral conversion? I think this can happen. In fact it seems to have been Augustine's situation at least for a time. But can a person have a moral conversion without an intellectual conversion? I think this also can happen. I am thinking of someone who might change his or her way of living but retains the same outlook that he or she had while committing serious sins. An example I am thinking of is a fundamentalist who believes in the completely literal interpretation of sacred scripture. I think such a person might undergo a moral conversion without undergoing an intellectual conversion.

Can a person undergo a religious conversion without undergoing either an intellectual or a moral conversion? My opinion is that someone who has a religious conversion might not have an intellectual conversion but it

---

seems to me a moral conversion would necessarily accompany a religious or spiritual conversion. Of course the ideal, I think, would be that all three types of conversion take place in a person's life. Followers of Christ are called to undergo what I would call "ongoing conversion." What I mean by the term "ongoing conversions" is that Christians are called to enter more and more deeply into the meaning of Christian faith, also called to avoid sin and most importantly called to fall more and more deeply in love with God. I see an "ongoing conversion" not so much as a radical change but rather as an intensifying and deepening of a person's life. In an "ongoing conversion" a person's conscience might be broadened, union with the Risen Lord might become more intimate and the person might become more receptive to the presence of the Holy Spirit.

Two different spiritualities have been part of my experience at least since college years. One I call eschatological Christian spirituality and the other I call incarnational Christian spirituality. Identifying these two spiritualities I have relied on many authors, perhaps the main one being Father John Courtney Murray, S.J., especially his ideas in his excellent book, *We Hold These Truths: Catholic Reflections on the American Proposition.*[39] In the book, Father Murray discusses two strong currents that existed in Christianity almost from the beginning. One he calls eschatological Christian humanism, the other incarnational Christian humanism. I have borrowed his distinction and applied it to spirituality. By spirituality I mean an image of self, of neighbor, and of God, and living out the

---

[39] John Courtney Murray, *We Hold These Truths* (New York: Sheed and Ward, 1960), pp. 175-196.

meaning of those images. So I don't think spirituality is the same as a philosophy. Spirituality includes the way you live. Reflecting on these two spiritualities and their implications for action I think can be very helpful in our efforts at living Christian lives. Neither spirituality contains any heresy; a person can be a good Christian embracing either spirituality.

The word eschatological comes from a Greek word meaning last. Eschatological spirituality emphasizes what have come to be called the four last things: death, judgment, heaven, or hell. This spirituality stresses that grace and heaven are gifts. No one has a right to either. The only important virtues are religious virtues such as faith, hope, and charity. There is strong emphasis on sin and also on the devil or the demonic. The basic vocation of the Christian should be waiting for the second coming of Christ. This world will eventually pass away. Father Murray claims that in the early Church there were some monks who spent their time weaving baskets and when they were finished they would unweave them and start all over again. The basic point was that it really does not matter what you do on this earth since everything will pass away. The symbol for the eschatological Christian is the Cross. If an eschatological spirituality is pushed too far there is a danger that the person might fall into the heresy of quietism which says that we do not have to do anything, that God will do everything. Pope Francis has commented that there was a time in Catholic spirituality that emphasized escape from the world but that now the emphasis is on engaging the world but always from a religious perspective.[40]

---

[40] Bergoglio and Skorka, *op. cit.*, p. 228.

In the early 1960s I heard a lecture by an outstanding Protestant moral theologian. After his talk I asked him what he thought about Pope John XXIII's encyclical *"Mater et Magistra,"* in which the Pope said that we should help poor countries not just out of charity but out of justice. The theologian made a statement like the following: "It is a great letter but it will not do any good. If you think that the rich countries will help the poor countries unless there is something in it for the rich countries, then you don't know anything about human nature. People are sinners." Looking back at that experience, I realize that the theologian probably embraced an eschatological Christian spirituality and had a very strong sense of sin.

An incarnational spirituality accepts that grace and heaven are gifts from God but stresses that in God's providence we are able to cooperate with God's grace. How we live does make a difference. There is a great difference between weaving baskets and running a business in which hundreds and hundreds can make a living wage. Of course there is a mystery of evil but Christ is stronger than the devil and we are called to cooperate in building the Kingdom of God. An incarnational spirituality recognizes that sin is everywhere, even in institutions, but it emphasizes that God's grace is also everywhere. The symbol for those who embrace an incarnational spirituality is not the Cross but the Risen Christ. If you push incarnational spirituality too far it might lead to secular humanism.

Can someone have both spiritualities at the same time? Though an individual can incorporate some aspects of each spirituality in his or her life, I don't think that someone can embrace each spirituality in its entirety at the same time because each spirituality has such a different emphasis. I think that the spirituality that was presented to me when I was a student in the major seminary in the 1950s was an eschatological spirituality and that this spirituality was illustrated powerfully in Thomas à Kempis' classic *The Imitation of Christ*, which the seminarians as a community read every day in chapel. Since Vatican II it seems to me that an incarnational spirituality has been presented in many Catholic books. Since the Council I have been trying to incorporate an incarnational spirituality into my life. There are signs that an eschatological spirituality is becoming popular again among some groups of Catholics. Whatever spirituality we embrace, it is good to reflect on how it is helping us to live as Christians.

Images of the Human Person and Images of the Living God

Many factors go into a person's spirituality. From schools to friends, from media to spiritual advisors, from scripture to liturgy, there are many realities that might influence how a person views himself or herself and how the person views God. The images we have of self and others are intimately linked to images we have of God and how we think of God can greatly influence how we think of ourselves.

From my study of the history of philosophy, I think I have discovered a pattern. When a thinker minimizes the powers of the human person in order to give credit to God, that view actually diminishes the greatness and mystery of God. When a thinker emphasizes the gifts of the human person, that view simultaneously provides a strong view of God's greatness. There is a parallel between the image of person and the image of God. As an illustration of this I would offer the thought of St. Thomas Aquinas. The Angelic Doctor had one of the strongest humanisms and also one of the strongest theisms. Other thinkers who had a seriously inadequate image of the human person seemed however inadvertently to set the stage for atheism.

Just around the time that I was becoming aware that some people I knew did not have any self-love, I came across what is called "A Litany of the Person." It may have been composed by the Trappist monk Thomas Merton.

A Litany of the Person

Image of God
born of God's breath
vessel of divine Love
after his likeness
dwelling of God
capacity for the infinite
eternally known
chosen of God
home of Infinite Majesty
abiding in the Son
called from eternity
life in the Lord
temple of the Holy Spirit
branch of Christ
receptacle of the Most High
wellspring of Living Water

heir of the kingdom
the glory of God
abode of the Trinity.
God sings this litany
Eternally in his Word.
This is who you are.[41]

I have been a Catholic all my life and a priest for half a century, but until a friend gave me a copy of "A Litany of the Person" about two years ago, I had never heard anything even remotely resembling it. There was a time in my life when I would have thought that such a litany was almost blasphemous. I would have thought that it fostered pride and that it focused too much on the human person and not enough on God. Now I think the litany is marvelous and I often give copies of it to others. What I love about the litany is that it highlights the most important truths about the human person. It says with many different phrases that God's love for us is beyond our imagination, and that what God has done for us and is doing for us reveals that love.

Is there anything in the litany which is not true? No. Though the litany focuses on the human person, each phrase also says something about God. The litany emphasizes, at least implicitly, that God and we, though distinct, are inseparable. Every statement we make about the human person is also implicitly a statement about God and every statement we make about God is also a statement implicitly about the human person. When I reflect on the litany, the person who comes to my mind is the great Catholic theologian Karl Rahner. His theology is a

---

[41] From Gethsemane Monastery, perhaps Thomas Merton.

profound reflection on the truth that God and human persons are inseparable because of God's loving involvement in our lives. I have read the litany many times and I find that I cannot pick out one phrase that is my favorite. Each one is revelatory of our dignity, our value, and our destiny in God's providential love.

At an early age I memorized the statement that we were made in the image and likeness of God but in the context of the litany the truth that we are images of God has taken on a deeper meaning for me. Perhaps every phrase in the liturgy can take on a deeper meaning if we meditate on the litany which is what I plan to do. This is not narcissism or navel-gazing but rather a way of entering more deeply into relationship with God Who is blessing us beyond our capacity to imagine or conceive.

Looking at the various phrases I find it difficult to pick out favorites but at least at this moment, I find four speak to me in a special way:

- dwelling of God
- capacity for the infinite
- chosen of God
- abode of the Trinity

Tomorrow perhaps four different phrases will have a special meaning for me. I will find it difficult to take this litany seriously and yet not trust in God.

CHAPTER THREE

The Seductive Power of Beauty

Works of Art in Relation to Ultimate Beauty

God Is Ultimate Beauty, the source of all other beauty. When I studied undergraduate philosophy as a seminarian, I learned that God was ultimate Truth, the ultimate Good, unlimited Being and ultimate Beauty but somehow that image of God as Beauty was to a great extent displaced by God as Truth and God as the Good. God as Ultimate Beauty and all beauty being a sign of God's presence has only recently become one of the images that I frequently use when I think of God.

That beauty has become so important in relation to how I think about God is related to two philosophy courses that I teach at the University: "Philosophy and Literature" (subtitled "Meaning, Mystery and Metaphysics in the Catholic Novel") and "Philosophy and Film" (subtitled "Movies, Mystery, and The Divine"). In both courses the mystery of God is at the center of everything we read or view and everything we discuss in class. I am trying not only to help students read great Catholic literature and experience great films that deal with the human mystery but also to see these works of art in relation to the Divine Mystery Who is Ultimate Beauty. When

I first began to teach these courses I stressed the presence of God in the content of the particular work of art, whether it was a novel or a film. This would be the answer to the question "What is the film or novel about?" I thought of the plot as being the main way that the beauty of the novel or film mirrored Divine Beauty. Now I try to call the attention of the students to the presence of God as Beauty in what might be called the form and shape of the work of art. Put simply, I try to call the attention of the students to whether the work of art is or is not well done. If it is well done, then the beauty of that work mirrors the beauty of God, is a finite reflection of God as Beauty.

Everything that I have written about beauty can be explained and defended by philosophy, by human reason without any reference to Christian faith. If we look at the presence of beauty from the perspective of religious faith and theology then the importance of beauty becomes even more evident. The Risen Lord and His Spirit are present everywhere. Even art, for example novels and films, which do not seem to be in any obvious sense religious, can, through their beauty, open readers and viewers to the mystery of God, to Ultimate Beauty. Because of the presence of the Risen Lord and his Spirit the encounter with beauty may lead not merely to an intellectual experience but even to an encounter with God.

The Drama of Beauty

In Father Michael Paul Gallagher's *Faith Maps: Ten Religious Explorers from Newman to Joseph Ratzinger*, Father Gallagher fittingly subtitles the chapter he devotes to Hans Urs von Balthasar "the drama of beauty." He points out that though Balthasar initially agreed with the theological approach that used the human person as the starting point of theology, he ultimately rejected that approach because he believed that it did not give sufficient emphasis to the God of revelation reaching out to us through His Son. Commenting on Balthasar's approach to Christian revelation, Father Gallagher writes the following:

> *"The early volumes of Balthasar's work deal with the perception of God's beauty; a second phase goes on to explore the drama of our freedom in answering God's call. These two moments—of recognition and response—are central to the experience of faith as he understands it. Moving away from the intellectualism of the scholastic tradition, he looks to aesthetics, or the encounter with overwhelming beauty, as the model for recognizing God's love in Christ. Then distancing himself from the cold moralism of previous theology, he looks to the tradition of theatre that represents faith as the interaction of two freedoms (God's and ours). Christianity, he insists, is not primarily 'a communication of knowledge' but a revelation of 'God's action,' continuing the biblical drama between God and humanity."* [42]

Just about everything in Balthasar's theology appeals to me and I confess that I find it inspiring. That we are called to respond to overwhelming beauty is mind-boggling. God desires our response, our involvement in a great drama, not merely a great drama but THE great drama. The story of every person's life looked at from the most profound perspective involves an interaction between two freedoms, ours and God's. The initiative is

---

[42] Gallagher, *op. cit.*, p. 53.

taken by God. How we respond determines how we live and how we die.

Hans Urs von Balthasar began his academic career by looking for hidden traces of Christ in literary works. For more than 25 years I have been conducting an adult education course in which we read what I describe as Catholic novels. My definition of a Catholic novel is one whose theme is based on some Catholic dogma, moral teaching, or sacramental principle, and in which the mystery of Catholicism is basically treated favorably. The students and I have studied more than 150 Catholic novels. I never would have read or re-read these novels except that I was conducting the course. For both the students and me the course has been a provocative and inspiring experience.

The Drama of Christian Living

Father Gallagher writes:

> *"Balthasar's focus on beauty seeks to retrieve neglected dimensions in the experience of faith, insisting that God's revelation invites us to a kind of ecstasy akin to the experience of great art. But this beauty is not of this world."* [43]

Though I had read at least one book by Hans Urs von Balthasar and in recent years learned from some students of theology that he had become a favorite theologian among large groups of contemporary Catholics, I knew little about his theology until I read Father Michael Paul Gallagher's book *Faith Maps*.

Now that I have some understanding of what Balthasar was emphasizing, I am hoping I can incorporate his view

---
[43] *Ibid.*, p. 52.

of the Christian life not only into my own view but also into my efforts at living as a follower of Christ. What is obvious to me about Balthasar, and also theologian Karl Rahner, is that these men looked upon theology not only as an important intellectual discipline but also as a vision that can influence a person's life. Theology was not an ivory tower activity for them but rather a probing of the depth of human persons and of their Creator. For them, theology should make a difference in our lives, indeed, should make a most meaningful contribution to our lives.

Balthasar's emphasis on God as Beauty and his emphasis on the beauty of Christian revelation greatly appeal to me. I am also excited, and even inspired, by his use of theatre as a metaphor for the Christian life. Human existence is a drama and God is at the center of the drama. In this drama each of us has an essential part. I have come to believe that we often have a weak sense of how fundamental the roles are that each of us plays. God's involvement with every person is both mysterious and awesome. I cannot picture God's providential love and involvement with the entire human race. It is not merely that God is present but is actively present, challenging the freedom of people to be more loving and to cooperate in the building of God's Kingdom. I do not believe that God ever takes away the freedom of His creatures but I do believe that God's loving presence can challenge, motivate, and direct us. God is moving all of history toward a goal and each of us is vital in the human drama. There are no unimportant or insignificant people.

Though God's involvement in my life is also mysterious, I find it easier to imagine than trying to imagine God's involvement in all of history. My life is surrounded by a loving God and whether I think of God's loving presence or don't think of it, God is still present and loving me. It is relatively easy as I look back on my life to see what I take to be the influence of God. I can think of major decisions I had to make and I am confident that God helped me make those decisions.

Summing up Balthasar's vision, Father Gallagher writes the following:

> *"This remains a powerful but austere vision. Perhaps it can only be grasped within a certain contemplative wonder and silence, where revelation invites us to a recognition that 'all is grace'.... All the multifaceted aspects of the mystery—the love of the Trinity the shock of the Cross, the glory of Resurrection, the outpouring of the Spirit into our struggling history—all this richness calls for a simplicity of heart that receives and adores and is gradually transformed. Faith in the vision is indeed a Yes to a Yes. The first Yes is God's, steady, eternal and then embodied in Christ. The second Yes is ours, unsteady, unfocused, yet learning to live with a strength that is not ours."* [44]

All of us are involved in a great drama and we have one another as companions and supports. We also have God. Or rather God has us. Everything that God creates is good and beautiful. God cannot create anything that in no way is beautiful. This means that if we have the ability to see the traces of God in God's creation then we are surrounded by beings that are beautiful. Poets, mystics, and saints may be more aware of this than the rest of us.

---

[44] *Ibid.*, p. 56.

Pope Francis has recounted an experience he had that greatly increased the beauty in his life. The experience happened when he was seventeen years old. Getting ready to go out with his friends he decided to start the day by visiting the parish church. When he arrived at the church he met a priest whom he had never met previously. Because the priest seemed to be a deeply religious person, Jorge decided to go to confession to him. Jorge was surprised that the confession, far from being routine, awakened his faith. Through that confession it was revealed to the teenager that he wanted to become a priest. The following is Pope Francis' description of the experience:

> "Something strange happened to me in that confession. I don't know what it was, but it changed my life. I think it surprised me, caught me with my guard down. . . . It was the surprise, the astonishment of a chance encounter. . . . That is the religious experience: the astonishment of meeting someone who has been waiting for you all along. From that moment on, for me, God is the One who te primerea—'springs it on you.' You search for him, but He searches for you first. You want to find Him, but He finds you first." [45]

Pope Francis believes that it was not just the astonishment of the encounter which revealed his vocation to him, but the compassionate way that God called him. Apparently this became a source of inspiration for him in his ministry and may account for Francis' compassion for others. Though certain of his vocation he waited four years before entering the seminary. The confession expe-

---

[45] Ambrogetti and Rubin, *op.cit.*, p. 34.

rience added greatly to the beauty of Francis' life. For Francis faith is an encounter with Jesus Christ. More than anything this is what makes a life beautiful, namely an encounter with God who is Ultimate Beauty.

I find the expression "poverty of spirit" more meaningful than the expression "spirit of poverty." The latter term means to me that we shouldn't be too dependent on material things or on wealth. We should have a detachment that enables us to emphasize in our lives what is most important. Obviously the spirit of poverty is important, but I think that poverty of spirit is more important and suggests some central and profound truths about what it means to be a person.

Theologian Karl Rahner in his theology emphasized that God's Spirit is already present and active in every person. I find this truth very encouraging. What I find challenging is the task of helping people, myself included, to become more aware of the presence of the Spirit as they participate in the human adventure, as they act out the drama that is part of everyone's life. I think that one way of helping people become aware of the presence of the Spirit in their lives is to get them to ask questions, such as "Why am I here? What do I want out of life? Whom do I love and what do I do for my loved ones and why do I do it? What is important to me in my life?" Perhaps a better way to become aware of the Spirit's presence would be to get involved in working with dedicated believers for those less fortunate than us. The act of reaching out in service accompanied by people who are believers might help to make the presence of the Spirit more evident. If Rahner were alive, he might tell us that what is most important is that people come in touch with what is deepest in them and reflect on that depth. If the Holy Spirit is present then that presence should be somehow discernible.

Rahner thought that today many people lived at a distance from their own depths and he saw this as a spiritual malnutrition. If they can be helped to be in touch with their deepest experiences then they might see that going beyond themselves toward truth and love, being generous in serving others and courageously facing life's difficulties goes way beyond any selfishness. All of this is a sign of the Spirit's presence. It is true that Rahner believed that theology should have self-experience as its starting point but this does not mean that Rahner is shrinking God to fit the human person's experience. What Rahner was insisting upon is that experience of the depth of self is simultaneously an experience of God. God's presence to human persons is what gives persons their ultimate and most important meaning. If in reflecting on the mystery of the human person we leave out the presence of God then we're not reflecting on the really existing actual human person because God and the human person are tied together.

Falling in Love with God

Philosopher-theologian Bernard Lonergan's analysis of our society in so far as it presents obstacles to religious faith speaks to my experience. Often I meet people who either cannot ask important questions about the meaning of their existence in the world or who for some reason have decided not to deal with such questions. Reading Lonergan's insights into our society I have made a resolution to encourage people, especially those who no longer attend the Eucharist, to ask themselves questions about what they believe and why. I plan also to ask them what they believe about the Eucharist. I have to admit I am stunned by the number of people I know who once regularly attended Sunday Eucharist but now almost never attend.

Lonergan thought we should try to reach a level of human authenticity. This involves realizing that our freedom means we are responsible for what we do as human persons. It is not too much to insist that we are in charge of our lives and the responsibility is awesome, perhaps even frightening. Of course there are many persons and events that influence us. I think immediately of my family and the schools I attended. Freud claimed that between the ages of three and six our basic personality was formed for life. Amazing view! It's all over by the time we reach six years of age! I disagree but I have to admit that families play an incredibly important role in people's lives. For many the schools they attended also played a big role in their growth or, unfortunately for some, in their decline. Lonergan thought that the strongest force in our lives should be love and he referred to falling in love as an extremely important experience in our lives. Commenting on Lonergan's vision Father Gallagher wrote the following:

> "*The climax of this adventure has not been mentioned; it involves the peak of our freedom where another reality enters the scene. That reality is love. Lonergan speaks of the event of falling in love as opening a person to a new state of 'being-in-love,' and of how this new horizon 'takes over' as the source of one's whole life. The experience of love anchors a person's energies; it is the contrary of a life of drifting. . . . Of*

course love can take different forms. There is a love of intimacy between people, and there is also a 'being in love with God' which 'can be as full and as dominant, as overwhelming and as lasting an experience as human love.' " [46]

Lonergan pays special attention to the religious experience of being in love with God. For the Canadian Jesuit this is the highest fulfillment of our capacity for self-transcendence. I find especially beautiful Lonergan's insight that faith is a knowledge that comes about through religious love. I know that for much of my life, and perhaps this is typically a problem for aggressive Americans, I thought of my efforts to grow closer to God as picking myself up by my own bootstraps and somehow on my own deepening my relationship with God. Perhaps this error is tied to the model that is often presented in our society of the "self-made man." Gallagher writes the following about Lonergan's view of faith:

*"Lonergan locates this recognition as the summit of a long adventure of human self-transcendence, where the burden of achieving gives way to the surprise of receiving, . . . to the overwhelming surprise of being loved by God. To know this with mind and heart is faith." * [47]

I believe we can never reflect too often or too deeply about the amazing truth that God is in love with us. The same God Who is creating the universe loves each of us.

---

[46] Gallagher, *op. cit.*, p. 69.
[47] *Ibid.*, p. 71.

Transformative Relationships

The greatest gifts we receive in our lives are the relationships we have. Think of the gift that parents can be to their children. They influence us physically, emotionally, and even spiritually. I believe very deeply in freedom, but I don't think being free means we cannot be influenced by others. The love we receive in our lives can actually help us to be more free. Because of that, parents have a tremendous opportunity to liberate their children, to help their children grow in freedom. I have come to believe so strongly in freedom that I think the holiest person in the world is also the freest person in the world.

When I was very young, whenever friends of my parents visited our home, they commented on how much I resembled my father. I recall looking in the mirror frequently trying to see how I looked like my dad and could see no resemblance. Now when I look in a mirror, my father is staring back at me. If I could look at my relationship with God the way I look in a mirror, I suspect I would find that my parents played an important role in the way I do or do not respond to God's presence in my life. We are free, but we are not alone in the world and others can affect us.

To a lesser extent, we are also probably formed and shaped by our brothers and sisters. Recently I have been thinking about my relationship with my sister, who died fifty years ago, and have come to see in a new way that much of the joy of growing up was tied to the presence of my older sister. Even as I am writing, I am thinking of what an important presence she was throughout my life right up to the moments of her final illness and death. To

say she was a blessing would be an enormous under-
statement.

I can only imagine the way spouses influence one
another. Two people who are mysteries to themselves
and to one another, trying to sustain a love relationship
for life, are involved in one of the great human adventures. Observing married couples I know, I can detect
some of the ways that their love relationship has changed
them, but my knowledge is just surface. Probably the
spouses themselves are not aware of how much their
relationship has transformed them. Though it is certainly
not the same as a marital relationship, the relationship
between two close friends can be life-changing. What do
friends give one another? In a deep friendship, they give
themselves. Imagine a very serious conversation
between two close friends. They may be exchanging
what is most important to them, their deepest needs and
desires and dreams. Their relationship may also challenge their consciences, expanding and deepening them,
and helping them to understand grace and sin more profoundly.

If all these relationships can influence us so deeply,
what about our relationship with Christ? We Catholics
believe that the Risen Lord can be encountered in the
sacraments. We believe that every Sunday at a Eucharist
the perfect offering of Christ to His Father is present, and
we can participate in that offering. We believe that when
we receive the Eucharist, this is not just looking back at
the Last Supper, some mere exercise of our memory.
Rather we believe that Christ Himself comes to us under
the appearance of bread and wine.

Everyone Has a Vocation

It is not clear to me whether I have a radically new image of God, different from previous images I had, or whether it is more a matter of emphasis. The "new image" is of God as constantly and dynamically active in my life and in everyone's life.

Many factors have contributed to my current image of God, factors as varied as celebrating the Eucharist, giving homilies, engaging in spiritual reading, having discussions with a spiritual director, celebrating the sacrament of reconciliation both as a confessor and as penitent, philosophizing both in class and in my room about the mystery of God and, perhaps especially, private prayer. One contributing factor was thinking about the meaning of vocation for a homily I had to give at a Sunday Eucharist. Preparing that homily moved me to think of God as a dynamic presence in everyone's life. God's active presence is a constant.

There are at least two meanings of vocation, meanings that are related though not identical. One meaning is what Catholics usually are referring to when they speak of a vocation: a spiritual call to priesthood or the religious life or marriage. Though a person can have a spiritual call to the single life, I don't think Catholics usually intend to include that when they speak of a vocation. That is unfortunate because the single life can be a marvelous vocation, a vocation that can lead to all sorts of opportunities to do good, opportunities that may not be available to a celibate priest or a religious. All the vocations that are intended with this meaning involve a life commitment. I suppose what has happened in my understanding of priesthood, religious life, marriage, and the single life is that I see that every one of these might be described as a "work in progress." Of course there is some finality to being ordained or in taking vows, but what I see more clearly than I saw previously is that God is constantly active in a person's life even after the person has made a life commitment. I suspect that, without realizing it, I had slipped into a kind of "deism," picturing God as a bystander in relation to our lives, perhaps an interested bystander, but a bystander nevertheless. I now think of God as always involved, always actively loving.

This brings me to the other meaning of vocation. Everyone is called by God. What I am thinking of is the call that every person receives, the call to enter a deep love relationship with God. Everyone is called—not only Catholics, not only Christians, not only those who believe in God, but everyone. Even agnostics and atheists are called. God's love reaches out to everyone. One of the great mysteries is that God, Who holds the universe in existence, wants a love relationship with everyone. Salvation and damnation hinge on whether a person says "Yes" or "No" to God's invitation. Pope Francis' frequent references to our journey and our path refer to us answering God's call. Everyone is on a journey with the Holy Spirit, a journey in which we are trying to respond deeply and with courage to God's call. We are being called by a God who loves us beyond our imagining. The Pope has commented with great honesty on his own journey, his own response to God's call:

> *"What hurts me the most are the many occasions when I have not been more understanding and impar-*

tial. In morning prayers, in supplications, I first ask to be understanding and impartial. I then continue asking for many more things related to my failings as I travel through life. I want to travel with humility, with interpretative goodness. But I must emphasize, I was always loved by God. He lifted me up when I fell along the way, He helped me travel through it all, especially during the toughest periods, and so I learned. At times, when I have to confront a problem, I make the wrong decision, I behave badly, and I have to go back and apologize. All of this does me good, because it helps me to understand the mistakes of others." [48]

---

[48] Ambrogetti and Rubin, *op. cit.*, p. 47.

CHAPTER FOUR

The Power of Story

"From a Catholic perspective at least, Christianity . . . underwrites those very properties of the novel, without which there is no novel; I am speaking of the mystery of human life, its sense of predicament, of something having gone wrong, of life as a wayfaring and pilgrimage, of the density and linearity of time and the sacramental reality of things" [49]

"People without hope not only don't write novels, but what is more to the point, they don't read them. They don't take long looks at anything, because they lack the courage. The way to despair is to refuse to have any kind of experience, and the novel, of course, is a way to have experience. The lady who only read books that improved her mind was taking a safe course—and a hopeless one. She'll never know whether her mind is improved or not, but should she ever, by some mistake, read a great novel, she'll know mighty well that something is happening to her. . . .

"The type of mind that can understand good fiction is not necessarily the educated mind, but it is at all

---

[49] Walker Percy, *Signposts in a Strange Land* (Edited with an introduction by Patrick Samway. New York: Noonday Press, Farrar, Straus and Giroux, 1991), pp. 177-178.

times the kind of mind that is willing to have its sense
of mystery deepened by contact with reality, and its
sense of reality deepened by contact with mystery." [50]

A number of experiences have led me to a renewed interest in the Catholic novel and to a deeper appreciation of its importance and the special contribution it can make to the Catholic community as well as to the wider reading public outside that community. Because every Catholic novel is about grace, every Catholic novel is about gift.

Several years after Vatican II during a conversation with a teacher of English at a Catholic high school with very gifted students, I learned that the teacher had a course in which he had the students read novels by Ernest Hemingway, William Faulkner, and F. Scott Fitzgerald. Interested and impressed by what the students were being exposed to, I suggested to the teacher that he might try giving a course on the Catholic novel, a course that might cover some of the great Catholic novels of the 20th century. The teacher showed absolutely no interest. The impression given was that such a course would be too narrow and parochial. Another experience was a meeting with a young lady who had graduated from a Catholic college, having majored in English. I was stunned to discover that the graduate not only had never read Graham Greene or Evelyn Waugh, she had never heard of them. This incredible discovery, that someone majored in English at a Catholic college and yet never heard of Greene or Waugh led me to inaugurate a Catholic novel course at St. John's University and shortly after that to begin an adult education course on the Catholic novel for the Brooklyn Diocese,

---

[50] Flannery O'Connor, *Mystery and Manners* (New York: Farrar, Straus and Giroux, 1957), pp. 78-79.

a course that over the years has covered over 150 Catholic novels. For me the course has become a kind of mission, indeed an apostolate extending to lectures at parishes, papers at scholarly conferences, and courses and discussions on television. For many, even many who read a great deal, the Catholic novel remains, unfortunately, a treasure hidden in a field. One reason that the Catholic novel has been neglected and continues to be neglected is that we live in a death-of-God culture, a post-Christian culture in which many intellectuals, those who put out the newspapers and magazines, create the plays and the films, write and review the books including novels, have bought into the philosophical vision known as secular humanism. It is a vision that underlies a great deal of contemporary fiction, painting, theatre, film, newspapers and journals of opinion. The contrast between contemporary art and previous ages was strikingly illustrated to anyone who attended the Metropolitan Museum of Art's Vatican Treasures exhibit several years ago. After viewing the magnificent evidence of faith in works of art for several centuries right up to the 20th century, a viewer had to be struck with the barrenness of the room dedicated to the art of the twentieth century. The ages of faith had passed.

Because of its widespread influence it seems a brief review of the basic tenets of secular humanism is in order. The philosophy is based on several assumptions, none of which are proven and none of which a Catholic consciousness would believe could be proven. The first is that there is nothing but matter; spirit does not exist. Human thinking and choosing can be explained materially. Evolution, which was not guided by some Creator because there is no such entity, is a chance process which happened to produce human beings. The way that some secular humanists articulate this is: "There are causes but no reasons," meaning that there is no Supreme Intelligence guiding the process. In fact intelligence appears very late in the evolutionary process, probably more than thirteen billion years after the process began. Because there is no intelligence behind the process there is no Divine Providence or a Divine Plan. How could there be since there is no God?

What some secular humanists find especially attractive about materialism is that it abolishes the temptation to dualism that has plagued Western thought since Plato (428BC—347BC) and was given a renewed life by Rene Descartes (1596-1650). For the secular humanist there is no problem which should receive more emphasis, the soul or the body, the natural or the supernatural, this world or the next world because there is no soul, no supernatural, and no next world. There is only the body, the natural, and this world. There need be no debate about reason and religious faith because there should be no religious faith. For the secularist, religious faith is merely superstition. That there is no life beyond the grave moves the secularist to devote his or her efforts to make this world a better place. That there is no reward in heaven frees the secular humanist from the temptation to do good because he or she will be rewarded in some future heavenly existence. While secular humanists might agree with religious believers that love is the most wonderful human activity, the secularists would confine love and its rewards to this side of the grave.

In his novel *The Plague* the atheistic existentialist Albert Camus dramatizes powerfully the attitude of the secularist toward love, suffering, and death. Dr. Rieux, an atheist, and Father Paneloux, a Roman Catholic priest, are working side by side in a hospital battling the plague. When a child dies they are both shaken. After Rieux reacts angrily to the child's death, this is the dialogue that follows:

> *"(Paneloux) 'Why was there that anger in your voice just now? What we'd been seeing was as unbearable to me as it was to you.' Rieux turned towards Paneloux.'I know. I'm sorry. But weariness is a kind of madness. And there are times when the only feeling I have is one of mad revolt.'*
>
> *" 'I understand,' Paneloux said in a low voice. 'That sort of thing is revolting because it passes our human understanding. But perhaps we should love what we cannot understand.'*
>
> *"Rieux straightened slowly. He gazed at Paneloux, summoning to his gaze all the strength and fervor he could muster against his weariness. Then he shook his head.*
>
> *" 'No, Father. I've a very different idea of love. And until my dying day I shall refuse to love a scheme of things in which children are put to torture.*
>
> *"We're working side by side for something that unites us—beyond blasphemy and prayers. And it's the only thing that matters."* [51]

In a culture imbued with a secular humanistic outlook it may be difficult for the Catholic writer to find an audience for the Catholic novel. This was a strong concern for Flannery O'Connor and Walker Percy. It moved O'Connor to state:

---

[51] Albert Camus, *The Plague* (Translated from the French by Stuart Gilbert. New York: The Modern Library, 1948), pp. 196-197.

*"When you can assume that your audience holds
the same beliefs you do, you can relax a little and use
more normal means of talking to it; when you have to
assume that it does not, then you have to make your
vision apparent by shock—to the hard of hearing you
shout, and for the almost-blind you draw large and
startling figures."* [52]

The problem is not just that a secular humanist might
not be drawn to a Catholic novel but that a secular
humanist critic might not even understand one.
However, it is not just a secular humanist culture that has
presented a problem for the existence of the Catholic
novel. The tide change in Catholic consciousness represented and to some extent caused by Vatican II also presented a problem. In her excellent study *The Vital
Tradition: The Catholic Novel in a Period of Convergence,* Jean
Kellogg has chartered the rise and at least temporary
decline of the Catholic novel. Kellogg argues persuasively that the Catholic novel thrived before Catholics "con-
verged with secular society." She states succinctly her
argument:

*"Only a novel whose mainspring of dramatic
action depends upon Roman Catholic theology, or
upon the history of thought in one of the world's large
Catholic communities, or upon 'development' in
Newman's sense is regarded as contributing to the
flowering of a major literary achievement that began
to break down with the end of the nineteenth century
and that tapered off—perhaps ended—when Roman
Catholics, in the phrase now so widely used, 'joined*

---

[52] O'Connor, *op. cit.*, p. 34.

the modern world' after the Second Vatican Council." [53]

There is no doubt that many Catholics were, and some perhaps still are, confused by the changes emanating from Vatican II. Kellogg, who put out her book in 1970, felt that Catholic self-understanding in relation to secular culture had moved from convergence to confluence, to a relation to secular culture that made it difficult to distinguish Catholic self-understanding. In an attempt to be relevant to secular culture had many Catholics lost their self-identity? Kellogg thought so and wrote:

> *"For great numbers of Catholics, confluence by the mid 1960's became so complete that they were no longer sure what the true Catholic essence was. The primary and defiant Catholic emphasis on the spirit, which for so many generations had generated the creative spark between the Catholic communities and the secular environment, virtually ceased."* [54]

Certainly as might be expected with developments of the Church's self-understanding there have been changes in the Catholic novel and for a brief time it may have appeared that the Catholic novel had disappeared not to return. We actually have a kind of "case history" that indicates both the power of the Catholic novel and a change in one Catholic's self-understanding that evolved into an embrace of secular humanism. This "case history" is Richard Gilman's provocative and moving autobiographical *Faith, Sex, and Mystery*. Gilman moved from a bel-

---

[53] Jean Kellogg, *The Vital Tradition: The Catholic Novel in a Period of Convergence* (Chicago: Loyola University Press, 1970), p. 1.

[54] *Ibid.*, p. 228.

ligerent skepticism to Catholic faith to a nearly total state of disbelief. About his journey into the Catholic Church, Gilman reports what a strong influence Catholic novels had on him and how after he left the church in a state of unbelief his experience of the novels was very different. Comparing the two experiences Gilman wrote:

> *"I wanted to hear about God then, an abstraction at the time, as he has become again. And he was there, lurking in all these fictional worlds, more or less a factor in the plots, often an antagonist, and his presence there—His presence; I suddenly remember the usage of faith and even of journalism—had the effect of making him—Him!—more human, if I can put it in that bizarre way. Certainly it made Him more distinctive. He could fit into literature, I thought, He wasn't just a value, even the Supreme one, He wasn't merely sublimity or the Good or the Truth or the Way, none of which was of any use to me at the time. He was someone, a character not wholly unlike all the others. . . . When I was preparing to write I discovered some etymological facts I should have known long ago: that the word 'narrative' comes from the Latin for 'to tell' and the word 'tale' is from the Anglo-Saxon or Middle English 'talu' one of whose chief meanings is 'speech.'*
>
> *"I looked up those words because I wanted to confirm my suspicion that the peculiarly intense quality of attestation, of bearing witness, that I'd found in those novels long ago, was an aesthetic matter as much as a religious one and that in fact their being works of literary art was just what gave them their credibility as spiritual testimony."* [55]

---

[55] Richard Gilman, *Faith, Sex, Mystery* (New York: Simon and Schuster, 1986), pp. 79-81.

After he had moved from Catholic faith to secular humanism, Gilman reported that it was precisely the religious dimension of the Catholic novels that seemed to him the weakest part of the stories. Of course if we were to excise the religious dimension from a Catholic novel there would be no story.

Gilman's experience is a vivid example of how the Catholic vision and the secular humanistic vision are radically different. There is no way that you can be a Catholic and a secular humanist. How much the pervasiveness of secular humanism in the twentieth century caused an erosion of Catholic consciousness so that the creation of Catholic novels became difficult, we will leave to historians and to more scholarly studies. Perhaps Kellogg was a bit too pessimistic. Though there has been a shift and so the Catholic novels of Alice McDermott are different from the Catholic novels of Graham Greene. Catholic novels were written by the late Walker Percy and are still being written as the works written by McDermott, Ron Hansen, Valerie Sayers, Mary Gordon and others illustrate.

If we reflect on the covenantal relationship that Catholics believe was initiated by God with the human race then an important role that the Catholic novel can play in our society can be appreciated. A narrow understanding of Divine Revelation, which I confess I once had, sees Divine Revelation as a set of answers that God sends from heaven, answers to all of life's vexing problems. This view looks at Divine Revelation almost as a book that God sent us with solutions to live by. I was sufficiently naïve to think of it as a catechism that God sent down to serve as a guidebook through life. As I became a bit more intellectually sophisticated I did not think of it as a catechism but rather as a theology textbook commenting on and unveiling the meaning of life's mysteries. We thought of Divine Revelation primarily as an information event, as something the human race was told. Connected with this notion was that faith was primarily an intellectual enlightenment that enabled a person to believe the information that God has presented. Of course this understanding of Divine Revelation and faith is terribly narrow and misses the exciting and indeed inspiring dimension of both.

A broader and deeper understanding of Revelation is held by Catholic theologians today, an understanding that can shed beautiful light on our daily experience. Theologian Edward Dunn expresses the contemporary Catholic understanding of Divine Revelation succinctly and clearly:

> *"God's gracious self-disclosure reaching out to humans as an invitation as well as promise to participate in God's own life of unfathomable love, mediated to us through persons, nature, history, everyday experience, and in an ultimate way, in and through God's very Word, Jesus Christ."* [56]

God did not have to reveal Himself. This is a gracious act. If we ask why God would do this probably the only answer we can come up with is because God is Love and Love wants to share. The self-disclosure of God is both an invitation and a promise and this is a much more marvelous understanding of Revelation than thinking of it as primarily imparting information. God invites us to enter into His own life of love, a love that is beyond our com-

---

[56] Edmond J. Dunn, *What is Theology?* (Mystic, Connecticut: Twenty-Third Publications, 1998), p. 42.

plete comprehension. God's invitation comes to us through God's Word and all other mediators are secondary and dependent on the mediation of Christ. But we should remember that there are secondary and subordinate mediators and Dunn mentions persons, nature, history, and everyday experience. We can add under the general heading of everyday experience the experience of art and more specifically the reading of the Catholic novel. The experience of Revelation, the hearing of God's invitation is a religious experience. Are we equating an artistic experience with a religious experience? No, but I think reflection on the two types of experience, their distinction and the possible overlapping in the life of an individual is worthy of serious reflection.

By a profound artistic experience we mean an experience of beauty through some work of art, for example a painting, a statue, a piece of music, a novel. But an artistic experience, no matter how deep, does not by definition necessarily point beyond itself to God. The profound artistic experience, which may even be supra-conceptual, that is beyond concepts and words to express, can stop with the artistic object. It does not necessarily go beyond experiencing the work of art. A religious experience which in a person may resemble an artistic experience in that it also is supra-conceptual, does point beyond toward God, indeed is an experience of God. That's why it is called religious. We can imagine an individual having such an experience in private prayer or at a Eucharist.

However, while artistic experience can be distinguished from religious experience by defining and describing them differently, in a person's life there may be considerable overlapping and blending. What I mean is that in the life of a person who is interested in art, the experiences the person has encountering works of art may start as only artistic experiences but move beyond those to experiences of the Divine. Revelation, God's loving invitation, is to everyone and so it is quite possible that this invitation can come to an individual through the experience of art, more specifically through the reading of a Catholic novel. The Spirit blows where it will! I believe this gives the Catholic novel a special importance, especially in a culture that does not regularly offer religious symbols. I am not suggesting that the Catholic novel be reduced to a tool for proselytizing. A Catholic novel should be a work of art and not reduced to a homily in story form. In discussing the novels in this chapter we are discussing novels that express "the literary word" that is, they are first and foremost literature, not sermons. They are significant works of art and so are worthy of attention on their literary merits and they express a special dimension of reality, indeed the most important dimension.

The working definition that I have used in choosing the novels for courses is the following: *A Catholic novel is one whose theme is based on some Catholic dogma, moral teaching or sacramental principle, and in which the mystery of Catholicism is basically treated affirmatively.* Of course "affirmatively" does not mean that every Catholic in the novel is a saint or that the human flaws in the Church are overlooked but that the Church's presentation of Christ's teaching is treated favorably. Flannery O'Connor's comment on the nature of a Catholic novel is essentially the same as mine. She wrote:

> *"The Catholic novel can't be categorized by subject matter, but only by what it assumes about human and*

*divine reality. It cannot see man as determined, it can-
not see him as totally depraved. It will see him as
incomplete in himself, as prone to evil, but as
redeemable when his own efforts are assisted by grace.
And it will see this grace as working through nature,
but as entirely transcending it, so that a door is always
open to possibility and the unexpected in the human
soul. Its center of meaning will be Christ; its center of
destruction will be the devil. No matter how this view
of life may be fleshed out, these assumptions form its
skeleton."* [57]

One Vote for Reading

I am trying to start a campaign, among my friends and
the college students whom I teach, to encourage reading.
Having talked with other college professors, I have the
impression that students no longer read for pleasure.
Reading is no longer one of the ways that they spend
leisure time. My guess is that with iphones, laptops,
MP3s, HDTVs, and cars there may be too many distrac-
tions. Reading may have tough competition from more
immediate pleasures. Whatever the reason, I think we
have a serious problem. I suspect that in relation to being
educated, as a way of shaping critical intelligence, a practice for expanding a person's horizon, there may be nothing as beneficial as reading. Add to that what seems to be
true: people who read are often very interesting people.

My sister was a voracious reader. She devoured books,
all sorts of books and she got through them quickly and
seemed to have a high level of comprehension. I recall an

---

[57] O'Connor, *op. cit.*, pp. 196-197.

incident that underlines for me how quickly she read and also how she seemed to easily retain what she read. I was scheduled to be one of two speakers at a communion breakfast. The day before the breakfast the other speaker called in sick. My priest friend, who had invited me, asked my sister if she would substitute for the ailing speaker. The day before the breakfast my sister speed read a book on Catholic Action and at the breakfast sounded like an expert!

I could offer many examples to indicate how a person's knowledge and experience are increased and deepened through reading. The one I tell my students is about my friend, who was a doctor and one of the most widely read men I have ever met. He read everything and was so intelligent that he forgot little of what he read. He was invited by an acquaintance to spend an evening watching slides of Europe that the man had taken on a recent vacation to Europe. As each slide appeared my doctor friend quickly identified what had been photographed and probably made a few comments about the history surrounding what appeared in the slide. Eventually the man showing the slides apologized. He said "Doctor, I am sorry. Here am I showing you these slides and obviously you have been to all these places that I visited." My friend said "I have never been to Europe. I have spent my entire life in Brooklyn." My friend had been to all the sites depicted in the slides through his imagination having been stimulated and educated through reading!

No one can experience everything directly but through reading we can experience vicariously. Great writers can help us have new experiences through the written word and the experiences through reading are often richer and more profound than if we were having the experiences directly. The great writers help us to see truths about human persons and even about God that we might not discover on our own. A theologian, who has marvelous insights into human nature, told me that he learned most of what he knows about human nature from reading literature. Years ago in an essay in *America*, the Jesuit magazine, Father Andrew Greeley wrote the following:

> *"Human artists see things more clearly than the rest of us. They penetrate into the illumination of being more intimately than do the rest of us. They want us to see what they see so that we can share in their illumination. They are driven to duplicate that beauty in their work. . . . The artist is a sacrament maker, a creator of emphasized, clarified beauty designed to make us see. Artists invite us into the world they see so that we can go forth from that world enchanted by the luminosity of their work and with enhanced awareness of the possibilities of life."* [58]

Everything that Father Greeley claims about artists applies to great writers. Dante, Chaucer, Dostoyevsky and many others can take us into new worlds. They can help us to see more deeply into the mystery of person and the mystery of God. Great literature can reveal the depth of human existence to us. In reading stories about others, we can come to a more profound understanding of ourselves. Great literature holds the mirror up to nature and in looking into that mirror we can see ourselves.

I am going to sketch six novels that I think are exceptionally good. I do this partially to offer six illustrations of

---

[58] Andrew Greeley, "The Apologetics of Beauty," *America*, September 16, 2000, p. 11.

what I have been claiming about great art, how it can reveal God as gift giver and human persons as gifted. I am also hoping to whet the appetite of those who may not have read these novels.

The Power and Glory (1940)

Graham Greene (1904-1991) at the age of 22, in order to know more about the religion of the woman he planned to marry, took instructions in the Catholic faith, though he had no intention of becoming a Catholic. However before his marriage in 1926, he did enter the Church.

Having already written a few novels, Greene had been trying since 1936 for a writing assignment that would take him to Mexico because he wanted to write about what he thought was the fiercest persecution of Catholics since the time of Queen Elizabeth. He got the assignment to report on religious persecution in Mexico in 1938, spent two months in Mexico and produced the book *The Lawless Roads* and then the novel which is his masterpiece, *The Power and the Glory*. For a short time the novel was published in the United States with the title *The Labyrinthine Ways*. That title was suggested by Francis Thompson's magnificent poem "The Hound of Heaven," the opening lines of which are:

> *"I fled Him, down the nights and down the days;*
> *I fled Him, down the arches of the years;*
> *I fled Him, down the labyrinthine ways*
> *Of my own mind,"* [59]

While the title's meaning may not have been immediately recognized by potential buyers, it did capture the

---

[59] Francis Thompson "The Hound of Heaven."

theme of the book. The novel is about flight and pursuit, about escape and capture.

Greene's priest, described in the story as a "whiskey priest," is the father of a child due to his sin of fornication. In Mexico in the 1930s persecution of the Church varied in severity from province to province. Eager to escape to a place where persecution of the Church was less violent with the hope of both physical safety and the opportunity to receive sacramental absolution for his sins, the priest has had several opportunities to escape. However, each time he jettisons his plans because word comes to him that some Catholic is seriously ill and needs a priest. Each time the priest, out of a sense of duty, knowing that he is the last sacramental minister in the province, chooses to stay, to put himself in danger of being caught and probably executed in order to help someone who needs a priest. The most dramatic example of this is when after he has crossed the border to safety, word comes to him that a criminal who is a murderer and a thief is dying and has asked for a priest. If the priest responds, he must go back to the area he has just fled. Certain that this is a trap, that the police will be waiting to arrest him, the priest goes back after reading the first four words of a note, supposedly written by the dying man. The words are "For Christ's sake, Father . . . "

The writing throughout the novel represents Greene at his best, which is to say near perfection. One has the sense that not a word is wasted nor out of place. Greene's creation of place and character is so successful that readers of the novel have told of visiting Mexico and of expecting to see the priest walking past. In trying to stamp out every vestige of the Church the authorities have created a country where there seems to be no life. Death hovers over the place. It is in this apparently God-forsaken spot that the priest has tried to bring God's sacramental presence. Throughout the novel Greene contrasts the priest with a young police lieutenant, a former Catholic who, having embraced Communism as the only hope to relieve the poverty of his people, now hates the Church which he sees as an opium for the people, an institution that provides false promises of a life beyond the grave while doing nothing to alleviate the people's poverty. The priest and the lieutenant are studies in opposites. The former is physically unattractive, unkempt and altogether not an impressive figure; the latter is a picture of strength and dedication, a man aflame with zeal for his cause. While the priest has failed in his commitment to live a celibate life, the lieutenant seems more ascetical and free of sensual temptations. His commitment expresses a man with a mission and he gives the impression that he would have no time for sexual dalliances.

On one level the novel is a typical thriller, an exciting tale of someone in danger being pursued, the kind of story that Greene masterfully told in novels such as *The Confidential Agent* and *The Ministry of Fear*. But *The Power and the Glory* is more of a theological thriller, an adventure in grace. Much more relentless than the lieutenant, God is the pursuer, the Hound of Heaven whose love is never withdrawn no matter what sin the pursued has committed.

A subplot involves a pious Mexican woman who reads saccharine stories about martyrs to her bored young son. Near the beginning of the novel the boy admires the lieutenant but eventually is drawn to the priest. Somehow the priest's presence has had an impact on the boy. One of the most dramatic scenes in the novel is the one in which the lieutenant and priest talk to one another the evening before the priest is scheduled to die before a firing squad. The lieutenant cannot understand why the priest did not take advantage of opportunities to save his life when he could have. Gradually the lieutenant is touched by the priest's sincerity, humility, and honesty. Describing himself the priest says:

> *"Why do you think I tell people out of the pulpit that they're in danger of damnation if death strikes them unawares? I'm not telling them fairy tales I don't believe myself. . . . But I do know this—that if there's ever been a single man in this state damned, then I'll be damned too."* And then Greene adds *"He said slowly, 'I wouldn't want it to be any different.' "* [60]

The lieutenant feels so sad for the priest that he tries to get an apostate priest to come to the prison to hear the condemned priest's confession. In doing this the lieutenant is breaking the law and risking his own career. The condemned priest who thinks he has driven God out of his life by his sins is a channel of God's grace for others. *The Power and the Glory* is probably the finest novel written in English that has a priest as its main character.

The Heart of the Matter (1945)

When Greene's *The Heart of the Matter*, appeared, Evelyn Waugh, distinguished author, fellow convert and friend of Graham Greene, wrote in the pages of *Commonweal* the following:

---

[60] Graham Greene, *The Power and the Glory* (New York: Penguin Books, 1940), p. 200.

> *"Of Mr. Graham Greene alone among contemporary writers one can say without affectation that his breaking silence with a new serious novel is a literary 'event.' It is eight years since the publication of* The Power and the Glory. *During that time he has remained inconspicuous and his reputation has grown huge."* [61]

Greene's reputation continued to grow so that his work became almost synonymous with the term "Catholic Novel." Eventually no book about the Catholic novel nor even an essay about the topic could be written without the mention of Greene's name. *The Heart of the Matter* is one of Greene's most interesting and controversial works. It also contains one of his most interesting protagonists. Images of that character may stay with the reader for some time after finishing the novel.

Greene chose as an epigraph for his novel the following words of poet Charles Peguy:

> *"The sinner lies at the very heart of Christianity. . . . No one is as competent as the sinner in matters of Christianity. . . . No one, unless it be the saint."*

The epigraph might be used for other Greene novels in which Greene engages in what might be called "theological paradox": the apparent sinner is closer to God than the apparently pious person.

Henry Scobie is a middle-aged Catholic deputy police commissioner of a district in Sierra Leone, a small British colony on the west coast of Africa. Though exceptionally honest, he is moved by the unhappiness of his wife,

---

[61] Evelyn Waugh in *Commonweal Confronts the Century: Liberal Convictions, Catholic Traditions* with an Introduction by Peter Steinfels, edited by Patrick K. Jordan and Paul Baumann.

Louise, to borrow from a corrupt merchant. Though the money borrowed enables him to send Louise on a holiday, the borrowing compromises his position as a government official. This may be the first false step on a moral journey that seems to end in tragedy. While Louise is away, Scobie reaches out in kindness to a nineteen-year old girl, Helen, who has lost her husband in a shipwreck. Having committed adultery with her, Scobie in a moment of weakness (or is it love?) pledges loyalty to the needy girl, a pledge he views as similar to his marriage vows to Louise. When Louise returns from vacation, Scobie feels he owes his love to both women and desperately does not wish to hurt either. Circumstances eventually lead him into a situation in which he will either commit a sacrilege by receiving the Host in a state of mortal sin or, by refusing to receive, cause Louise to be seriously suspicious.

It says something about Greene's skill as a writer that he makes this melodramatic situation real, exciting, and believable. One of the most dramatic scenes in the novel is when Scobie, believing he is sacrificing his own salvation, nevertheless chooses to make a sacrilegious communion. The following is a description of Scobie receiving:

> *"Father Rank came down the steps from the altar bearing the Host. The saliva had dried in Scobie's mouth: it was as though his veins had dried. He couldn't look up, he saw only the priest's skirt like the skirt of the medieval warhorse bearing down upon him: the flapping of feet: the charge of God. If only the archers would let fly from ambush, and for a moment he dreamed that the priest's steps had indeed faltered: perhaps after all something may yet happen before he reaches me: some incredible interposition. But with*

> *open mouth (the time had come) he made one last*
> *attempt at prayer 'O God, I offer up my damnation to*
> *you. Take it. Use it for them' and was aware of the pale*
> *papery taste of an eternal sentence on the tongue."* [62]

After the sacrilegious communion, Scobie feels he is damned. Besides being concerned not to hurt Louise or Helen, he is tortured because he is offending God Whom Scobie sees as completely vulnerable to Scobie's offenses. In one enormously touching scene Scobie sits at the back of the church, as Greene notes "as far as he could get from Golgotha," which Scobie believes he is submitting Christ to again. He thinks that because he is in mortal sin there's no use in praying and yet he says to God:

> *"O, God, I am the only guilty one because I've*
> *known the answers all the time. I've preferred to give*
> *you pain rather than give pain to Helen or my wife*
> *because I can't observe your suffering. I can only*
> *imagine it. But there are limits to what I can do to*
> *you—or them. I can't desert either of them while I'm*
> *alive, but I can die and remove myself from their blood*
> *stream. They are ill with me and I can cure them. And*
> *you too God—you are ill with me. I can't go on month*
> *after month insulting you. . . . You'll be better off if*
> *you lose me once and for all."* [63]

Scobie does not wish to offend Louise or Helen and so he chooses suicide but he chooses it primarily because he does not wish to offend God. It may be easy for a Catholic reader to judge that Scobie's conscience is twisted and confused but the reading of the novel is an extraordinary

---

[62] Greene, *The Heart of the Matter* (New York: Penguin Books, 1948), p. 209.
[63] *Ibid.*, p. 241.

experience. Greene's inordinate talent makes Scobie's dilemma and struggle not only interesting but even inspiring. The real presence of God seems to leap off the page. Strange as it may seem as Scobie thinks he is sinfully slipping away from the loving presence of God in his life, the reader may become more aware of the loving presence of God in Greene's text. Theologian/publisher/author Frank Sheed once remarked that Graham Greene wrote as though the headline on the morning paper was "Son of God died for me." Sheed's description perfectly fits *The Heart of the Matter*.

The End of the Affair (1951)

It is unlikely that any reader who finds the first few pages of *The Power and the Glory* slow or uneventful until the realization dawns that Greene is sketching a Godless terrain would have a similar reaction to the opening paragraphs of the *The End of the Affair*. In the first two paragraphs of the novel readers are exposed to the conflicts that are dramatized and developed in detail in the body of the novel. The narrator, Maurice Bendrix, a novelist, announces that the story is about hate much more than love and indicates that the moment he chooses, arbitrarily or not, as the moment to locate the beginning of the story, was a time when he and Sarah and Henry Miles were lucky enough not to believe in God. Bendrix's story is a record of how Sarah and he move from disbelief in God to hatred of God and finally to love of God, in the person of Sarah, perhaps to sainthood.

Sarah Miles, who frequently has been unfaithful to her husband, Henry, a rather dull civil servant, falls passionately in love with Bendrix. During the London blitz, a bomb hits the building in which they have met for clandestine love-making. Maurice has left the bedroom seconds before the bomb hits to see if it is safe for Sarah to return to her home. Sarah goes downstairs looking for Maurice, and finds Maurice apparently dead, killed by the impact of the bomb. Returning to the room where they were making love, she kneels at the bed and desperately asks the God she does not believe in to let Maurice live, and promises that if Maurice lives she'll try to be good, that she'll even give Maurice up forever if God lets him live. She is still kneeling when Maurice enters the room. Believing that God has restored Maurice's life, that a miracle has happened, Sarah feels obliged to keep her promise. The rest of the novel deals with the mysterious loving presence of God drawing Sarah into a love relationship of which her affair with Bendrix was an image. The epigraph that Greene chose from Leon Bloy expresses one of the themes of the novel:

> *"Man has places in his heart which do not yet exist,*
> *and into them enters suffering in order that they may*
> *have existence."*

Though Bendrix is the narrator of the story, one of the extremely effective tools that Greene uses in his exciting and inspiring novel is Sarah's diary. For a time Bendrix, and we the readers, believe that the reason Sarah has ended the affair is that she has taken up with another human lover. Jealous, Bendrix hires a private detective, Parkis, a conscientious if not especially intelligent character, whose presence in the novel provides some comic relief. When Parkis obtains the diary both Bendrix and we learn why Sarah terminated the affair.

The pages in *The End of the Affair* that are filled with Sarah's reflections from her diary are a special revelation of Greene's skill as a writer. The voice is female, very different from Bendrix's voice. It's uncanny that Greene is able to make this transition from one narrator to another so smoothly. Never do we have the impression that Sarah's diary is written by a male. What the pages from the diary also provide, as Sarah expresses the pain of loss she has in giving up Maurice, is the increasing appreciation she has of God's unlimited love for her as well as her own experience of falling more and more deeply in love with God. The diary seems like a brief female version of Saint Augustine's *Confessions*. In fact Sarah's writing seems a record of mystical experience. The following is an example:

> "*Did I ever love Maurice as much before I loved You? Or was it really You I loved all the time? Did I touch You when I touched him? Could I have touched You if I hadn't touched him first, touched him as I never touched Henry, anybody? And he loved me and touched me as he never did any other woman. But was it me he loved, or You? He was on Your side all the time without knowing it. You willed our separation, but he willed it too. He worked for it with his anger and his jealousy and he worked for it with his love. For he gave me so much love, and I gave him so much love that soon there wasn't anything left, when we'd finished, but You. . . . You were there, teaching us to squander, like you taught the rich man, so that one day we might have nothing left except this love of You. But You are too good to me. When I ask you for pain, You*

> *give me peace. Give it to him too. Give him my peace—he needs it more.*" [64]

In another section of the novel Bendrix comments that the saints have used the words of human love to describe their experience of God and he wonders if the terms used in prayer and contemplation can be used to explain the intensity of the love that a man feels for a woman. *The End of the Affair* is about the intensity of both loves, the finite leading to the Infinite. In view of this the title of the novel can be understood in two ways. The obvious meaning refers to the termination of the love affair because of the promise and the miracle. The more important meaning relies on the word "end" in the title meaning goal or purpose. This would indicate that the title refers to the love affair between Sarah and Maurice pointing toward and leading to the love of God. Hence even the novel's title expresses an Augustinian theme: "Our hearts are restless until they rest in Thee."

Reflecting on the insights into both human sexual love and love of God that fill the pages of *The End of the Affair* makes it easy to understand why no less a literary personage than William Faulkner described the novel as "One of the most true and moving novels of any time, in anybody's language."

Brideshead Revisited (1945)

Prior to writing *Brideshead Revisited*, Evelyn Waugh had achieved a well-deserved reputation as a talented satirist with novels such as *Vile Bodies* and *Scoop*. Though satire can be serious business, Waugh tried something even

---

[64] Greene, *The End of the Affair* (New York: Penguin Books, 1951), p. 123.

more serious and of greater depth with *Brideshead*. The novel is one of the best Catholic novels of the 20th century, a genuine masterpiece. The eleven-part television series may be the finest ever to appear on the tube. Though the television adaptation was written by John Mortimer, a professed agnostic, it faithfully and successfully dramatizes the Catholic themes in the novel. As a stylist Waugh may have no equal among 20th century authors. The novel may remind contemporary readers how beautiful the English language can be when it comes from the pen of a master. In *Brideshead*, Waugh tries what would seem nearly impossible and succeeds: charting the providential presence of God drawing people, who may have temporarily drifted, back into a loving relationship with Himself.

The subtitle of the novel is a summary statement of its plot: *The Sacred and Profane Memories of Captain Charles Ryder*. The novel has a prologue and an epilogue which cover events on the same day during the Second World War. Captain Charles Ryder and his fellow soldiers, engaged in training exercises, come upon a beautiful mansion called "Brideshead." The encounter stirs up memories of important moments in Ryder's life that were spent at "Brideshead" and his relationships with several members of the aristocratic family who have inhabited the estate. Those memories make up the substance of the novel. In choosing the word "Brideshead," Waugh is using St. Paul's notion of Christ as the head of the Church and the Church as Christ's bride. As the novel progresses the symbolism of the mansion suggesting both Christ and His Church becomes increasingly evident and significant. "Brideshead" is so central to the plot that it almost seems to be a character, perhaps the most important character.

Ryder's introduction to the aristocratic family comes through Sebastian Flyte when the two are undergraduates at Oxford. Charles recalls:

> *"I knew Sebastian by sight long before I met him . . .*
> *he was the most conspicuous man of his year by rea-*
> *son of his beauty, which was arresting."* [65]

Through his friendship with Sebastian, Charles eventually meets the other family members: an older brother, Brideshead, a staunch Catholic but rather rigid, a sister, Julia, who like Sebastian is strikingly beautiful, a teenage sister Cordelia, Lady Marchmain, a devout Catholic, and Lord Marchmain, a convert to Catholicism, who by the time Charles meets him has long left the Church, his wife, and the mansion and lives with his mistress, Cara, apparently as far from Lady Marchmain as feasible.

At one point in the novel Cordelia mentions to Charles, who is an agnostic, a Chesterton Father Brown short story in which the priest explains how he caught the criminal. Cordelia says:

> *"Father Brown said something like 'I caught him' (the*
> *thief) 'with an unseen hook and an invisible line which*
> *is long enough to let him wander to the ends of the*
> *world and still to bring him back with a twitch upon*
> *the thread.'"* [66]

The line, when applied to the providential presence of God in the lives of the principal characters in the novel, can be taken as the theme of *Brideshead Revisited*: God lets sinners wander far but eventually brings them back with

---

[65] Evelyn Waugh, *Brideshead Revisited* (Boston: Little Brown and Company, 1945), p. 28.
[66] *Ibid.*, p. 220.

a "twitch upon the thread." This is what happens to Sebastian, to Lord Marchmain, to Julia, and even to Charles Ryder.

The journey of each in the novel is fascinating and calls attention to how God's love is often, if not always, mediated through others. There is reference in the novel to forerunners, to someone being a pointer toward a greater love. Love of Sebastian is a forerunner of the love that Charles eventually has for Julia, and the love that Charles and Julia have for one another becomes a forerunner for the love they ultimately have for God. The attractive and seductive beauty of the mansion "Brideshead" is a forerunner for Christ and His Church. The beauty of the mansion, though finite, points toward the infinite beauty of God: to paraphrase Rudolf Otto's phrase for the holy, beauty is a mystery that is awesome and overpowering but also fascinating and seductive.

One of the more touching descriptions of God's love is given by Cordelia, who, now 26 years of age and physically unattractive, has spent some time in a convent and can seem to be living in Charles' phrase "a thwarted life." She is telling Charles of a visit she made to see Sebastian, now a seemingly hopeless alcoholic who has attached himself to a monastery in Tunis as a kind of doorkeeper. Saddened by the image of Sebastian as an alcoholic living off the charity of the monks, Charles says that he imagines that Sebastian does not suffer to which Cordelia replies that she thinks he suffers a great deal and that someone really cannot be holy without suffering. Agnostic Charles is stunned by the word "holy" and wonders how it will all end. Confident that she knows, Cordelia tells Charles that Sebastian will return to the monastery from one of his drunken sprees and will indicate by the mere flick of an eyelid that he is conscious and welcome the last sacraments and will receive them. She concludes, "It's not such a bad way of getting through one's life."

Confused by Cordelia's remarks, Charles does not come to understand until he experiences "the twitch upon the thread" shortly after God has drawn back Lord Marchmain and Julia, both of whom had given up the practice of the faith, Julia through a love affair with Charles. Lord Marchmain's deathbed conversion is probably the most famous scene in the novel. Having earlier refused the priest, Marchmain is asked by the priest to give some sign that he accepts God's forgiveness. Ryder is present with Julia as the priest anoints the seemingly unconscious Marchmain. The following words are Ryder's:

> "Then I knelt, too, and prayed: 'O God, if there is a God, forgive him his sins, if there is such a thing as sin' . . . .
>
> "I suddenly felt the longing for a sign, if only out of courtesy, if only for the sake of the woman I loved, who knelt in front of me, praying, I knew, for a sign . . . . All over the world people were on their knees before innumerable crosses, and here the drama was being played again by two men—by one man, rather, and he nearer death than life; the universal drama in which there is only one actor.
>
> "The priest took the little silver box from his pocket . . . touching the dying man with an oily wad; . . . Suddenly Lord Marchmain moved his hand to his forehead; I thought he had felt the touch of the chrism and was wiping it away. 'O God' I prayed, 'don't let him do that.' But there was no need for fear; the hand

*moved slowly down his breast, then to his shoulder,
and Lord Marchmain made the sign of the cross."* [67]

By the end of *Brideshead Revisited* all the principal characters have revisited "Brideshead!"

Mariette in Ecstasy (1991)

In his *A Stay Against Confusion: Essays on Faith and Fiction*, Ron Hansen wrote:

"Writing, then, can be viewed as a sacrament insofar as it provides graced occasions of encounter between humanity and God." Noting that symbols help us discover what possibilities life offers, us, Hansen wrote:

"Writing will be a sacrament when it offers in its own way the formula for happiness of Pierre Teilhard de Chardin. Which is: First, be. Second, love. Finally, worship. We may find it's possible that if we do just one of those things completely we may have done all three." [68]

Mariette in Ecstasy tells the story of a 17-year-old girl, Mariette Baptiste, who in 1906, enters a strict contemplative order, "the Sisters of the Crucifixion," of which her 27-year-old sister, Mother Celine, is the superior. Four months after Mariette enters the priory, which is named "Our Lady of Sorrows," Celine dies of cancer. The next day, Christmas, Mariette begins to experience the stigmata, which Mariette considers a gift from God. The rest of the novel deals with mystery in at least two senses. The first is the one all Catholic novels deal with, the mystery

---

[67] *Ibid.*, p. 338
[68] Ron Hansen, *The Stay Against Confusion* (New York: HarperCollins Publishers, 1991), p. 13.

of God's loving presence in the lives of people. The second is unique to Hansen's novel, the mystery surrounding Mariette's experience of the stigmata, which raises questions about whether Mariette's wounds are an authentic replica of Christ's wounds, whether Mariette is deliberately deceiving the sisters and the convent's chaplain, Father Marriott, or whether Mariette is a sexual hysteric. Because of the clever way that Hansen constructs his story, sprinkling it with what may be clues to the truth or merely "red herrings" planted to keep the reader in a state of doubt, readers may find themselves changing their opinion every few pages right up to the last page of the book, which may contain the most provocative last line of any Catholic novel.

There is much in the novel that a contemporary reader might find strange. The invitation to Mariette's reception into the religious order reads like a wedding invitation, stating that God and the Virgin Mary are inviting people to attend the spiritual wedding of their Son Jesus to Mariette. There is a flashback early in the novel to Mariette at the age of four standing before a statue of Jesus and touching her private parts. Later when she is in the convent she explains that while praying she sits on her fingers in order to prevent sins against purity and has done this since she was a child. At home on the morning she is scheduled to enter the convent she stands naked before an upright floor mirror, and while admiring her phsyical beauty, including her full breasts, which she has seen men admire, she says *"Even this I give You."* [69] Mariette's relationship with her father seems unusual, if not strange. A doctor, he conducts the required physical

---

[69] Ron Hansen, *Mariette in Ecstasy* (New York: HarperCollins Publishers, 1991), p. 9.

examination before she enters the convent. At one point when Mariette and he are in the room in which Celine is dying, Hanson writes of Mariette *"She feels his eyes like hands. Enjoying her. She knows their slow travel and caress."* [70] At one point while working in the convent kitchen Mariette places her hands into scalding hot water. When asked if she was thinking of the souls in purgatory, Mariette says that she just wanted to hurt.

Hansen builds up suspense by interspersing in the narrative comments from an investigation that the chaplain is conducting, questioning the sisters about what they think of Mariette's presence in the convent. Some of the sisters think that she is a saint and that her presence is a great blessing for the convent. Others have a more negative view. Mother Raphael, who had been Mistress of Novices when Mariette entered the convent and who became superior when Celine died, has great difficulty with Mariette and her exceptional experiences. How much Mother Raphael's judgments are objectively based and how much they are due to Mother Raphael's own problems in the spiritual life are questions that will probably occur to anyone reading the novel.

Hansen introduces Satan into the novel, first as a spiritual presence in Mariette's cell but then also under the disguise of a nun going to confession and as the author of a letter in which Mariette is seriously criticized. Placing the devil as a character in a novel, which Walker Percy and Flannery O'Connor have also done, seems an especially daring and risky act in a death-of-God culture. However Hansen succeeds admirably, especially in the confession scene which is truly frightening.

---

[70] *Ibid.*, p. 97.

There are at least two sections describing what has come to be called the "Dark Night of the Soul," a state of severe aridity and loss of emotional consolation in prayer, a condition suffered by some of the saints such as John of the Cross, and apparently experienced for close to thirty years by Mother Teresa of Calcutta. There is also a marvelous description Mariette gives of her experience of ecstasy. The following are excerpts:

> *"In prayer I float out of myself. I seek God with a great yearning, like an orphan child pursuing her true mother. . . . A sweet power is drawing me, a great and beautiful force that is effortless and insistent. I flush with excitement and a balm of tenderness seems to flow over me. And when I have gotten to a fullness of joy and peace and tranquility, then I know I have been possessed by Jesus and have completely lost myself in him. Oh, what a blissful abandonment it is. . . . Every feeling I have is of his kindness and heavenly love. Every dream I have had is realized in Him."* [71]

In commenting on the research he did in writing *Mariette*, Hansen mentioned the writings of St. Thérèse of Lisieux and Thomas Merton, as well as also reading about some who have experienced the stigmata such as Gemma Galgani. He also read the medical diagnosis of Padre Pio's experience of the stigmata. Hansen notes that he allowed his factual sources *"to be distorted and transmuted by figurative language, forgetfulness or by the personalities of the fictional characters."* [72] Whether readers do or do not think that the writing in *Mariette in Ecstasy* is sacramental,

---

[71] *Ibid.*, p. 128.

[72] Ron Hansen, *The Stay Against Confusion* (New York: Harpercollins Publishers, 1991), p. 9.

Mariette is a fictional character who will not be easily forgotten.

The Moviegoer (1961)

Walker Percy lost both his parents while he was a teenager, his father committed suicide and his mother died in an automobile accident. A cousin of Walker's father, affectionately known as "Uncle Will" adopted Walker and his two younger brothers. A lawyer and an author, Uncle Will, an ex-Catholic who had embraced Stoicism, was a strong positive influence on Walker's life. Having received a medical degree from Columbia University College of Physicians and Surgeons, Walker, during his internship at Bellevue in 1942, contracted tuberculosis. His recuperative period during which he read serious novels by Dostoevsky and Tolstoi and the existentialist philosophy of thinkers such as Camus, Sartre, Heidegger, Kierkegaard, and Marcel, changed his life. He underwent an intellectual conversion and saw that science, of which he previously had been greatly enamored, could not say anything meaningful to a person facing death. His intellectual conversion was followed by a religious conversion when he and his wife, after studying religion for a year, became Catholics in 1947.

Never returning to the practice of medicine, Percy wrote some philosophical essays that appeared in scholarly journals. Believing that he had something important to say and wishing to reach a wider audience, Percy decided to write novels. The first was *The Moviegoer*. Given Percy's intention, getting what he had to say to a wider audience than he might through scholarly essays, there could be a danger that, instead of creating art, he might merely be writing homilies in story form for prose-lytizing purposes. Not to worry. Percy's six novels are genuine works of art and *The Moviegoer* is literature of the first order. The novel might be described as a novel of ideas. Though it is not necessary to have an academic background in philosophy in order to enjoy this book, it may well call readers to reflection on the meaning of personal existence, to look upon person as mystery rather than as problem. Indeed the novel might provoke readers to reflect on several important life issues.

The novel, set in the late 1950s, covers one week in the life of Binx Bolling, who lives in the suburb of Gentilly in New Orleans. It is the week before Ash Wednesday, which will be Binx's 30th birthday. Binx is the moviegoer of the title and he seems to be caught in a purposeless existence, in what Percy has called the malaise, which is a banal existence, flat with no depth, no adventure, no challenge. Someone in the malaise may play a role but because there is no authenticity, the person is alienated from self and others. It can result in boredom to the point of numbness but also to anxiety. Binx knows that something is missing from his life and so he is on a search. He believes that the search is what others would be on if they realized the aimlessness that pervades their being. Binx recognizes that *"to become aware of the possibility of the search is to be onto something. Not to be onto something is to be in despair."* [73] The epigraph for *The Moviegoer* is a quotation from the Danish Christian existentialist Soren Kierkegaard: *" . . . the specific character of despair is precisely this: it is unaware of being despair."* Binx's self-awareness leads him to the search and enables him to avoid despair. In all his novels Percy takes

---

[73] Walker Percy, *The Moviegoer* (New York: Vintage International, 1960), p. 13.

on various "isms" that pervade contemporary culture, one of which is consumerism. Early in *The Moviegoer* of which he is the narrator, Binx describes himself. He mentions his job, his apartment, his wallet that is filled with identity cards, library cards, and credit cards, that he subscribes to *Consumer Reports* and because of that owns an air conditioner, a television set, and a long-lasting deodorant. Binx's description of himself is an accurate description of a consumer but somehow the "self" seems to be missing. Sensing this Binx goes to movies to find meaning but he finds films let him down because they only help for a time. So in his search he must look elsewhere.

He does not find what he is looking for in the trivialization of sex that is part and parcel of the so-called sexual revolution. Though he regularly has affairs with his secretaries, he finds that by the time they break up they are bored with each other. At one point in the novel Binx is on a trip to Chicago with Kate, his cousin by marriage, who seems to suffer from a kind of neurasthenia. He tries to have sex with her but finds that for the experience to have any depth of meaning more is required than the mere physical act. As is revealed in many of Percy's novels, there is a mystery to sex that transcends the merely physical but also includes it. Sex illuminated by commitment can reveal to us our deepest selves. This is how Binx describes the failed liaison with Kate:

> *"The burden was too great and flesh poor flesh, neither hallowed by sacrament nor despised by spirit (for despising is not the worst fate to overtake the flesh), but until this moment seen through and canceled, rendered null by the cold and fishy eye of the malaise— flesh poor flesh now at this moment summoned all at*

once to be all and everything, end all and be all, the
last and only hope— quails and fails." [74]

There is at least a hint that Binx's search will only be
fulfilled by religion and that is exactly what happens. We
learn in the Epilogue that Binx has married Kate and is
ready to lovingly be available to her for the remainder of
their lives. This life commitment is linked to another.
When asked if his half-brother, Lonnie, who has died, will
be healthy when Christ raises people on the last day,
Binx's "Yes" indicates that Binx Bolling's search has
reached its goal!

Reflecting on the three novels by Greene, Waugh's
masterpiece and *Mariette*, I am struck by how much pain
and suffering are in these books. Years ago, Greene's novels were criticized for lacking Christian joy. I don't feel it
is a valid criticism. The pain and suffering in all these novels have to be understood under the light of Christ's suffering and Resurrection. I am reminded of an insight into
suffering which Pope Francis received when he was twen-
ty-one years old and seriously sick with pneumonia and
suffering enormous pain. The young man didn't care for
the platitudes that friends offered such as "This will
pass." However, the words of Sister Dolores, the nun who
had prepared him for his First Communion, shed for him
new light on his suffering. She said: "You are imitating
Christ." In the young man this was an insight into how to
confront suffering in a Christian manner that apparently
has helped the Pope throughout his life. He has said:

> *"Pain is not a virtue in itself, but you can be virtu-*
> *ous in the way you bear it. Our life's vocation is ful-*

---

[74] *Ibid.*, p. 200.

fillment and happiness, and pain is a limitation in that search. Therefore, one fully understands the meaning of pain through the pain of God made Christ." [75]

---

[75] Ambrogetti and Rubin, *op. cit.*, pp. 24-25.

CHAPTER FIVE

God in Film

TWO thousand years ago when a teenage girl said "Yes" and the Son of God entered her womb, the Incarnation happened. It is still happening today in the sense that God's Word is still being spoken. One important way that it has been spoken in the past and can be spoken in the future is through art and specifically through film. This chapter will suggest why theology and spirituality should take film seriously, very seriously.

It is not surprising that the Pope likes Italian Neorealist films. He commented:

> " . . . the Italian Neorealist movies, which my parents introduced me and my siblings to. They wouldn't let us miss a single movie with Anna Magnani or Aldo Fabrizi, which, as with the operas, they would explain to us. They'd give us two or three basic notions to get us started; then we'd head off to the neighborhood cinema, where they'd show three movies in a row." [76]

---

[76] Ambrogetti and Rubin, *op. cit.*, p. 154.

Distinguished Italian film directors such as Vittorio De Sica and Roberto Rossellini took their cameras into the streets and filmed life as it was lived in post-war Italy. I can't help wondering what an impact Rossellini's *Open City* had on the future Pope, with its marvelous depiction of a dedicated priest played by Aldo Fabrizi. This is a film every seminarian should see.

One of Pope Francis' favorite films is *Babette's Feast*. His commentary on it may qualify him as an excellent film critic:

> *"It's true that at times, the question of suffering has been over-emphasized. I'm reminded of one of my favorite films,* Babette's Feast, *where you see a typical case of taking prohibitive limits to the extreme. The characters are people who live a form of exaggerated puritan Calvinism, to the point where they experience the redemption of Christ as a negation of the things of this world. When the novelty of freedom arrives in the form of an abundant meal, they all become transformed. In truth, this community didn't know what happiness was. They lived their lives crushed by pain. They were devoted to the gray side of life. They feared love."* [77]

Many sources could be used to sketch a philosophy of person. The key point that I wish to stress is that person is relational. A person can decide where to relate and how to relate but cannot decide not to relate. To be relational is the nature of person. To be a person is to be open *to*, present *to*, in dialogue *with*. This is because human consciousness is always consciousness of. It is impossible just to be

---

[77] *Ibid.*, pp. 25-26.

conscious. There is always an other that is the object of consciousness. This is true even of self-consciousness. What a person is conscious *of*, open *to*, in dialogue *with* is meaning. The sum total of the network of meanings or set of meanings that are real to a person can be called the person's world. Though our worlds can overlap, no two persons have exactly the same world. A person's relationship with his or her world is dynamic. The person's world is either deepening and broadening or unfortunately, narrowing and perhaps becoming shallow. The human will is oriented toward the Infinite Good and the intellect is naturally ordered to the whole of being as intelligible. The human person can be totally satisfied with nothing less than the Divine. There is an inexhaustible depth to the self because of our openness to the Infinite. This view of the human person is quite exciting. The more deeply we are able to penetrate the world, the more deeply we can enter into ourselves and the more deeply we can enter into ourselves the more comprehensive becomes our relationship with what is other than the self. There is a kind of spiral between self-presence and outward openness to other. Norris Clarke, S.J. writes:

> "And, paradoxically, the more intensely I am present to myself at one pole, the more intensely I am present and open to others at the other. And reciprocally, the more I make myself truly present to the other as an 'I' or self, the more I must also be present to myself, in order that it may truly be I that is present to them, not a mask." [78]

This view of the human person as dialogical and as growing in presence to others and in presence to self,

---

[78] Clarke, *op. cit.*, p. 76.

reaches a new level of importance when Christian revelation is brought into the picture. Everything that has been
said about personal existence takes on a new and more
profound meaning when the entrance of God into history
is considered. Of course what we think Divine Revelation
is will affect what we think faith is. I confess that for much
of my life I had a rather narrow understanding of faith
that matched my understanding of Divine Revelation. I
thought of faith as largely a knowledge affair. It was an
enlightening of our minds that enabled us to believe the
answers or message that God had revealed to us. It is of
course much more than that. I rely again on Edmond
Dunne who offers the following definition of faith:

> *"Faith is our freely given, graced response to God's
> invitation to a loving relationship that begins in pre-
> conceptual form but takes its cognitive form in creeds,
> preaching, prayer, doctrines, and dogmas of the faith
> community, and calls us to a discipleship of worship,
> personal transformation and action on behalf of jus-
> tice."* [79]

To put it simply, faith is our saying "Yes" to God's invitation to a loving relationship. This acceptance of God's
invitation calls us to worship and to conversion and to act
on behalf of justice. Because the "yes" happens at the pre-
conceptual level, it is at least possible that some persons
who consciously have not accepted Christ have in fact
said "yes" to God. Why they have not consciously accepted Christ may be due to many factors among which
might be their upbringing and education, the secular
humanistic society in which they live, the scandals in

---

[79] Dunne, *op. cit.*, p. 53.

Christian churches right up to present-day scandals, the unimpressive Christians they know or have met. Whatever the reasons, it is possible that some whom we have described in the past as having "baptism of desire" or as "anonymous Christians" may be sincerely following their consciences and in fact may be very close to God.

God's invitation is constant. It did not only take place two thousand years ago. God has not withdrawn the invitation. If by "secular" we mean some place where God's invitation is not being offered, there is no such place. Either Revelation is happening while I am writing this book and you are reading this book, or all of us are wasting our time. Because God's Revelation is constant, our "yes" can take place at any time and in any place. We hope our "yes" will happen at a Eucharist or in the Sacrament of Reconciliation or in formal prayer but it can take place actually at any time. Because this invitation can be mediated through nature, our "yes" can happen looking at the Grand Canyon or at a starlit sky. Because it can be mediated through persons, our "yes" can take place when we listen lovingly to someone, when we forgive someone, when we visit the sick or perform other deeds of kindness. The invitation can come through art and more specifically through film.

Pope John Paul II wrote a magnificent statement about the importance of art, his "Letter to Artists." He wrote:

> *"God therefore called man into existence, committing to him the craftsman's task. Through his 'artistic creativity' man appears more than ever 'in the image of God,' and he accomplishes this task above all in shaping the wondrous 'material' of his own humanity and then exercising creative dominion over the uni-*

*verse which surrounds him. With loving regard, the
divine Artist passes on to the human artist a spark of
his own surpassing wisdom, calling him to share in
his creative power. . . .*

   *"Every genuine art form in its own way is a path
to the inmost reality of man and of the world. It is a
wholly valid approach to the realm of faith, which
gives human experience its ultimate meaning. That is
why the Gospel fullness of truth was bound from the
beginning to stir the interest of the artists, who by
their very nature are alert to every 'epiphany' of the
inner beauty of things."* [80]

Pope John Paul II highlighted for us the importance of
art. It can be a mediator of God's loving invitation to us.
In relation to the topic of theology and communication I
could focus on the truth present in art and the good that
is present in art but instead I have chosen the transcen-
dental, beauty. St. Thomas' definition of beauty was *"Id
quod visum placet,"* "that which when seen pleases." The
Angelic Doctor did not mean only seen with the eyes but
seen with the mind. Because God is Unlimited Beauty, it
is impossible for God to create a being that is not beautiful. Even creatures that may not immediately seem
beautiful to us, such as cockroaches or tarantulas, have a
beauty which we might discover if we take the time to
consider them more carefully. As a revelation of God as
Beauty, art has a special power. In language that is almost
lyrical Andrew Greeley has beautifully expressed the
attraction of beauty:

---

[80] Pope John Paul II, "A Letter to Artists (April 4, 1999) Online Edition – Vol. V, No. 5:
July-August.

"Contemporary Catholic theology, whether it be of the Balthasarian or Rahnerian variety, agrees that of the three transcendentals inherent in Being—Truth, Goodness, and Beauty—the Beautiful is primary in that we encounter it first. It overwhelms us, enchants us, fascinates us, calls us. As we ponder it, we see that it is good and are attracted to the Goodness it represents. Finally, bemused by the appeal of goodness, we discover that it contains truth, and we listen to the Truth we hear from it. . . .

"We live surrounded by God's beauty. Sometimes we notice it. Sometimes, all too rarely perhaps, the beauty all around us invades us, stops us in our tracks, explodes within us—a stately cactus outlined against a rose-gold sunset, the faint light of a winter sun on a smoothly frozen lake, the smell of mesquite in the air after a rainstorm, a goofy smile on a child's face as she tries her first brave steps, the touch of a friendly hand, an erotically attractive human body, a meteor shower on a late summer night, a chocolate malted with whipped cream, monarch butterflies flying along a beach on their way home. All are grace and grace is everywhere, often not noticed but still there." [81]

An especially provocative treatment of beauty as a way of thinking about God as Beauty is in John Haught's *What is God? Some New Ways to Think of God*. In presenting new ways to think about the Divine, Haught employs Rudolf Otto's famous phrase to describe the holy: *mysterium tremendum et fascinans*, "a mystery that is overpowering and fascinating." Haught applies this phrase to depth,

---

[81] Greeley, *op. cit.*

future, freedom, beauty, and truth. Beauty is a mystery and is frightening because it can overpower us, call us out of ourselves, cause an ecstatic reaction in which we might lose control. Though it can be frightening, it is also seductive and alluring. It is impossible for someone to say honestly "I don't want any more beauty in my life." We have an insatiable desire for beauty. When we try to describe how our life is going, we really are describing how beautiful or how lacking in beauty our life is. Though we may not normally speak of trying to aestheticize our life, that is what we are always trying to do.

In his discussion of beauty Haught relies on Whitehead's insight that beauty involves the harmony of contrasts. Commenting on Whitehead, Haught writes:

> *"What makes us appreciate the beauty of things is that they bring together nuance, richness, complexity and novelty on the one side, and harmony, pattern and order on the other. The more 'intense' the synthesis of harmony and contrast, the more we appreciate their union. Nuance without harmony is chaos, and harmony without nuance is monotony. Beauty involves the transformation of potentially clashing elements into pleasing contrasts harmonized by the overarching aesthetic pattern of the beautiful object or experience."* [82]

What we are trying to do in our lives is make them more beautiful which means we are modeling our lives on God, Who is Unlimited Beauty. No beautiful finite object that we encounter totally satisfies us.

---

[82]   Haught, *What is God?* (New York: Paulist Press, 1986), p. 72.

Haught goes on to make an important point that I will use to stress the important role that great films can play in our lives. Haught writes:

"The identity of all of us is established by our interaction with the narrative context of our existence. Our sense of the meaning of our lives, if we are fortunate enough to be conscious of living meaningfully, is a gift of the narrative nest in which we dwell. The meaning of our lives is determined by the way in which each of us participates in an ongoing story. And where people today speak of their experience of meaninglessness, isolation, alienation, rootlessness, etc., such experiences can almost invariably be traced to an inability to find some meaningful story in which to situate their lives." [83]

Infinite Beauty is inviting us into a loving relationship. As Catholics we have many mediators through whom or through which Divine Beauty's invitation can come to us. We have built into us a desire for beauty and though no finite beauty can fulfill completely that desire, finite beauty can be a mediator to us, a channel to us of God's presence. There are many channels. One that theology and spirituality may have neglected is film. It has been pointed out by many that film, which was the art form of the 20th century and may be the art form of the 21st century, can include all the other arts in itself—painting, music, literature, theater, poetry. Perhaps one film will not change anyone's life but a diet of great films has to change us and transform us. Great films have an extraordinary beauty and they can serve as a sign of an invitation from Divine Beauty.

---

[83] *Ibid.*, p. 74.

Two ways that we can view a film as beautiful are as "that which when seen pleases" or as a "harmony of contrasts." The theme of a film can be beautiful. What it says about nature or human beings or God can be beautiful. At the center of the work of art is a beautiful insight or idea or message or whatever we wish to call it. Put it this way: at the center of the film is what the film is saying and what the film is saying may be very beautiful. It is a sign or finite imitation of Divine Beauty. The creator of the work of art might not think of his or her insights as finite imitations of God. Imagine an atheist who is a great artist. Obviously he or she would not think finite beauty is an imitation of Divine Beauty. In making judgments about the beauty or lack of beauty of a film's theme or insight, we bring into play our entire vision of reality. What our philosophy of person is, what our theology is will affect and influence our judgment. Because of my philosophy of person, I would judge that a theme that denies human freedom is not true and hence not beautiful. My theology might lead me to judge that a film that some might describe as religious is in fact presenting a very superficial or even erroneous view of God. I know one Catholic critic who thought Mel Gibson's *Passion of the Christ* was heretical because the Jesus it presented was not human. No human being could have endured the suffering that Gibson depicted. The main point I am making is that ideas, insights, themes can be more or less beautiful. When one is deeply beautiful, it is, to echo Haught's emphasis, a mystery that calls us out of ourselves, a mystery that is an imitation of Unlimited Beauty.

However we must not forget that a film is a work of art, not just a free-floating theme. Judgments about the material components are crucial. The artist cannot just have a brilliant insight. The artist must have the skill to express that insight in matter. With film the insight somehow has to be on the screen. Of course there are many artists that contribute to the making of a film—the author, the director, the actors, the music composer and arranger, the cinematographer, the set designer, the costume designer, the producer—just to name a few. If a film can be attributed to one artist then it would seem that the director is the most likely candidate. The director has to tie together all the contributions of everyone who has worked on the film. Anyone who works on a film can make a positive or negative contribution. We probably can recall films in which the story was weak or the actors were either miscast or inadequate or the music was more of a distraction than a benefit. Any piece of a film can strengthen or weaken the mosaic that the finished film is. In citing the director as usually the most important artist, I do not wish to minimize the contribution of other artists but only to note that if a film is to be attributed to one artist the director would seem to be the proper choice since he or she gathers together the contributions of all the other artists and fits them into the completed work.

In evaluating any film we have to consider not only how beautiful or lacking in beauty the theme or insight behind the film is. Equally important is to evaluate the material component of the film, the way that the theme or idea has been presented. How beautifully has the theme been presented? A film may have a beautiful theme but not be a beautiful film because the camera work detracted from the theme or the actors were terrible or the music drowned out the dialogue or some other part of the film was not beautiful. Of course the opposite might also happen. Different parts of a film might be beautiful such as the camera work or the acting or the music but the film is not saying anything significant. In such a case parts of the film might be beautiful but the film as a whole is lacking in beauty.

Artistic or aesthetic judgments are difficult to make. What I want to stress is that difficult as they are to make, we should make them. As a mediator of Divine Revelation film is a treasure that for theology and theologians may still be hidden in a field. The first step for theologians is to take films seriously. Years ago in one of the best books on film that I have ever read Roy Huss and Norman Silverstein called attention to an attitude toward film that may still exist among many:

> *"Since moviegoers do not have to be told what a movie is, critics seem presumptuous when they write about art. When they lay stress on cinematic details and employ technical terms, finding analogies between film and painting or literature, moviegoers find critics pretentious as well. The film is so clearly a part of one's growing up that one naturally looks down on those who make movies an experience comparable to listening to Beethoven, looking at Picasso, or reading Milton. The film is a Saturday afternoon entertainment. . . . On TV, movies are bedtime stories for adults in which problems, hard in life to get into and impossible in life to solve, absorb the interest of those who like hard problems and easy solutions."* [84]

---

[84]   Roy Huss and Norman Silverstein, *The Film Experience* (New York: A Delta Book, 1968), p. 1.

The view that films are nothing but escapist entertainment should be rejected if theology's and spirituality's dialogue with film is going to increase and improve. Through viewing great films and perhaps reading some guides, people may find a new, exciting channel of Revelation.

A warning may be in order. In looking at film we should not look only at the theme or message. A film should be viewed as a work of art and not only the beauty of its theme should be appreciated but also the beauty of the manner in which the theme is presented. Shrinking a film to nothing but a tool for proselytizing would be a big mistake. The matter or manner is as important as the insight when art is being experienced. This can lead to a strange phenomenon, a film that has a religious message but is very poorly done may be less of a revelation of God than a film that expresses doubt about the existence of God but is a very well-made film. The well-made film may reveal beauty in a way the "religious film" does not. As examples of films whose themes convey doubt about God's existence but are beautiful works of art and so reveal God through their beauty, I offer Ingmar Bergman's *The Seventh Seal* and Woody Allen's *Crimes and Misdemeanors*.

To try to make my remarks about Revelation and beauty more concrete I intended to offer a list of films that might illustrate my view of Revelation, beauty, and film. Within two or three minutes my list had grown to forty-five films. Rather than provide such a lengthy list I will discuss three films as examples of beautiful films that might serve as mediators of God's invitation to a love relationship. Each film is beautiful in terms of plot and theme and also beautiful as an incarnation of artistic insight, beautiful in the cinematic aspects that go to make up a film. The three films are George Stevens' *Shane* (1953), Elia Kazan's *On the Waterfront* (1954), and Robert Benton's *Places in the Heart* (1984), three American master-pieces by three outstanding American directors.

The story of *Shane* is similar in some ways to other Westerns. A stranger who is an ex-gunslinger, Shane (Alan Ladd) arrives at the Wyoming homestead of Joe and Marion Starrett (Van Heflin and Jean Arthur) and their young son Joey (Brandon de Wilde). Staying on as a hired hand, Shane is soon involved with the Starretts' efforts to preserve their home from a cattle baron, Ryker (Emile Meyer). Frustrated by Joe Starrett's refusal to leave, Ryker brings in a hired gun, Jack Wilson (Jack Palance) and plans to have Wilson kill Starrett. Risking his own life, Shane takes Starrett's place in the showdown, kills Wilson and Ryker and rides out of the valley.

The Technicolor film is visually glorious. But most interesting are the signs that Shane is a Christ-figure able to save the "holy family" of Joe and Marion and child. Shane first appears mysteriously riding down from the mountains and, as though to keep mysterious origins before us, Stevens has the beautiful mountains as a back-drop during many scenes. At the end of the film, wound-ed in the hand, Shane rides back into the mountains, hav-ing risked his life out of love for others. The wound in the hand suggests a wound of Christ. More importantly while many Western heroes ride off into the sunset, Shane rides off into the sunrise suggesting resurrection.

In the film, Shane has a strong appeal to all, both to men and to women. He is celibate and though there is a strong attraction between him and Marion their relation-ship remains chaste. Shane is ready to sacrifice himself for

the homesteaders who are losing their battle with the cattlemen whose greed and desire for power seem unlimited. The evil of the cattlemen is represented by Wilson and
against him the homesteaders do not have a chance.
Lloyd Baugh comments:

> *"To meet and defeat this level of evil which threat-*
> *ens individuals, society and a whole civilization, a*
> *particular moral hero is needed, a redeemer, a restorer*
> *of order, a bringer of grace and freedom, one who not*
> *only has the ability to act, the skill, the power, but also*
> *the moral courage, the spiritual freedom to risk all, to*
> *offer himself in redemptive sacrifice. The quadruple*
> *trumpet blast on the soundtrack when the newly-*
> *arrived stranger says to Starrett as they shake hands,*
> *'Call me Shane,' is Stevens' signal that the much-*
> *needed hero is Shane."* [85]

While some of the characteristics of Shane might apply
to many Western heroes, there is clearly another dimension to Stevens' hero. Chris Calloway (Ben Johnson), who
early in the film bullies Shane, has a conversion experience because of his experience of Shane. He terminates his
relationship with Ryker and warns Shane that Ryker
plans to have Wilson kill Starrett. Even Chris does not
understand what has happened to him. When Shane asks
him why he has changed, Chris says "I don't know.
Something's come over me."

Baugh insists on Shane's image as a Christ-figure:

> *"If Stevens allows the possibility of some degree of*
> *Christic identification in Shane because he acts as*
> *friend and defender of the downtrodden, as teacher*

[85] Lloyd Baugh, *Imaging the Divine* (Kansas City: Sheed and Ward, 1997), p. 161.

*and protector of the innocent, and because he is a free
man, giving and inspiring trust and love, then he certainly pushes this possibility further by creating
around his protagonist an aura of mystery, both for the
other characters in the film and for the viewers of the
film. Shane arrives as if out of nowhere, not even a
pack on his horse. His origins and recent past remain
almost a total mystery for the entire film. . . . His good
looks, his intelligence and sensitivity, his balanced
manner of speaking and acting, set him mysteriously
apart from all, as does his astonishing degree of freedom, generosity and selflessness. He is clearly a man
for others. His future, his destiny and concretely, his
departure at the end of the film, having completed his
mission of redemption, riding back up into the mountains whence he came, remain a mystery."* [86]

One of the clearest indications of Shane as a Christ-figure is Stevens' employment of a cross at the end of the
film. As Shane rides into town for the showdown with
Wilson, a showdown in which he is risking his life
because of his love and concern for others, Stevens brack-
ets the showdown scene with two dramatic shots of a
cross. The first is superimposed on the screen as Shane
rides into town to confront Wilson and this composite
shot is held for five seconds. The second is after the showdown, Shane rides past the same cross and wounded,
rides into the sunrise, an excellent image of resurrection.

The music in *Shane* adds greatly to the beauty and
power of the film. There is a different musical motif for
Marion, the villains, and Shane, and the one for Shane is

---

[86] *Ibid.*, p. 164.

played differently throughout the film depending on what is happening on the screen.

On the Waterfront tells the story of Terry Malloy (Marlon Brando) an ex-prizefighter longshoreman who unknowingly cooperates in the murder of a fellow longshoreman, Joey Doyle. Through the influence of Joey's sister, Edie (Eva Marie Saint) and a priest, Father Barry (Karl Malden) Terry's conscience comes alive and he says more than once in the film "There's more to this than I thought" indicating his reflection on the moral meaning of his life. Terry's older brother, Charlie (Rod Steiger), is the right hand man of "Johnny Friendly" (Lee J. Cobb) who is the crooked boss of the union. The centerpiece of the film, capturing both the theme and what happened to Terry as the film progresses, is a homily by Father Barry in the hull of a ship over the dead body of "K.O." Dugan, who was murdered because he was ready to testify against "Johnny Friendly" and the crooked union. Having promised "K.O." that if he stuck his neck out to testify against the union that he would follow up and do everything in his power to battle corruption, Father Barry in the hull of a ship makes the following remarks over Dugan's body to a large group of longshoremen including Terry:

> *"Some people think the crucifixion only took place on Calvary. They better wise up. . . . Dropping a sling on 'K.O.' because he was ready to spill his guts tomorrow—that's a crucifixion. And every time the mob puts the crusher on a good man—tires to stop him from doing his duty as a citizen—it's a crucifixion. And anybody who sits around and lets it happen— keeps silent about something he knows has happened*

—shares the guilt of it just as much as the Roman sol-
dier who pierced the flesh of Our Lord to see if He was
dead. . . . Boys, this is my Church! And if you don't
think Christ is down here on the waterfront, you've
got another guess coming! Every morning when the
hiring boss blows his whistle, Jesus stands alongside
you in the shape-up. He sees why some of you get
picked and some of you get passed over. He sees the
family men worrying about getting the rent and getting food in the house for the wife and kids. He sees
you selling your soul to the mob for a day's pay. . . .

"And what does Christ think of the easy-money
boys who do none of the work and take all the gravy?
And how does he feel about the fellows who wear hun-
dred-and-fifty dollar suits and diamond rings, on your
union dues and your kickback money? And how does
He, who spoke up without fear against every evil, feel
about your silence? You want to know what's wrong
with our waterfront? It's the love of a lousy buck. It's
making the love of the lousy buck—the cushy job—
more important than the love of man! It's forgetting
that every fellow down here is your brother in Christ!
But remember, Christ is always with you—Christ is
in the shape up. He's in the hatch. . . . He's kneeling
right here beside Dugan. And He's saying with all of
you, if you do it to the least of mine, you do it to me!
And what they did to Joey, and what they did to
Dugan, they are doing to you. And you. You. All of
you. And only you, only you with God's help, have the
power to knock'em off for good." [87]

---

[87] *On the Waterfront*, 1954.

During the homily Director Kazan frequently cuts to a close-up of Terry listening to the priest and being challenged by Christ.

Perhaps to emphasize the theme Kazan uses the symbol of the cross often in the film. Early in the film while Father Barry is urging the longshoremen to do something about the crooked union, there is a deep focus shot of a holy water font in the rear of the church and a cross is clearly visible on it. There is a crucifix in Edie's room. There are several scenes on the roof of apartment buildings and some of the television antennae form crosses. Another reference to the cross is the murder of Terry's brother, Charlie. His body is hung on a wall like a crucified body. As the story progresses, Terry is a living illustration of Father Barry's homily. Terry lives out Jesus' way of the cross. He is beaten and bloodied around the head. At Father Barry's urging he staggers to his feet to lead the longshoremen back to work, a clear sign that they will no longer take orders from "Johnny Friendly." Though similar to Moses leading his people toward the Promised Land, Terry's faltering steps and his fall on the way toward the work site is more reminiscent of Jesus' New Passover. The film ends with Father Barry and Edie, a clear symbol of St. John and the Virgin Mary at Jesus' suffering and death, viewing Terry's victory march.

Leonard Bernstein's music adds considerably to the tender scenes of love between Terry and Edie as well as the more violent scenes involving the mob.

On the Waterfront is an excellent example of many artists contributing to the beauty of a film. Actors Marlon Brando, Eva Marie Saint, Rod Steiger, Karl Malden, and Lee J. Cobb were never better than they are in this film. *On*

the Waterfront is the best of all Kazan films and he directed many fine films. The screenplay by Budd Schulberg is
outstanding. Jewish, Schulberg gives us in Father Barry
the best fictional priest in any American film. Schulberg
based the character on Jesuit Father Corridan, known as
"the waterfront priest." Looking back at his experience as
an advisor on the film, Father Corridan noted that there
seemed to be a mysterious presence on the set contributing to the creation of the film.

Places in the Heart, written and directed by Robert
Benton, takes place in a small town in Texas in 1930, the
town in which Benton grew up. As the film opens we hear
on the soundtrack the hymn "Blessed Assurance" being
sung.

> *"Blessed assurance, Jesus is mine!*
> *O what a foretaste of glory divine!*
> *Heir of salvation, purchase of God,*
> *Born of His Spirit, washed in His Blood.*
> *This is my story, this is my song,*
> *Praising my Savior all the day long.*
> *This is my story, this is my song*
> *Praising my Savior all the day long."*

There are brief shots of the church and of some of the
white and black inhabitants of the town. There is a brief
shot of each of the principals in the film, all the people
who will play an important role in the story.

Central to the story is Edna Spalding (Sally Fields), her
two small children and her husband who is the sheriff in
the town. After the montage of shots giving a glimpse of
some of the inhabitants in the town, the camera settles on
the Spalding family having Sunday dinner. While they are

eating, they hear several gun shots. The sheriff's deputy comes to the house and announces that there is a drunken Negro down by the railroad tracks firing shots. When the sheriff goes to investigate, he is accidentally killed by the Negro, who is subsequently killed, dragged through the streets and hung on a tree by some of the townspeople. The funerals for the two men are strikingly different, extending even to two different cemeteries, one for white people, the other for black people.

The remainder of the film is Edna trying to keep her house and children with almost no money to pay her mortgage. She takes in a blind war veteran Will (John Malkovich) to help with expenses and houses a black drifter, Moze (Danny Glover) to help with the seemingly impossible goal of making her field of cotton a money making proposition. A subplot involves her sister Margaret (Lindsay Crouse) and her husband, Wayne (Ed Harris) who is having an affair with a married friend of the family, Viola (Amy Madigan). Just about every imaginable human problem, both physical and emotional, strikes the family and Benton's camera captures all of them as the writer-director draws extraordinary performances from his cast.

Near the end of the film Margaret has discovered Wayne's infidelity with Viola and refuses to forgive him. Moze has been driven away by members of the Ku Klux Klan but not before, like the biblical Moses, he has been a leader helping his adopted family to succeed with the cotton field.

The film ends with the most beautiful Eucharistic scene in the history of American film. On the soundtrack we hear the hymn we heard at the beginning of the film. It is being sung at a communion service taking place in the local church. Margaret and Wayne are sitting in the front pew. The minister reads aloud St. Paul's hymn to charity. As the minister is reading, Margaret reaches over and touches Wayne's hand. His eyes fill with tears. Margaret has forgiven him. Then the minister reads the account of the Last Supper. The communion plate and the small cups of wine are passed among the parishioners. We see Margaret and Wayne and several parishioners take Communion. The camera slowly pans faces in the congregation as parishioners receive the bread and wine. Suddenly we are shocked to see Moze at the end of the pew with white people passing the communion plate. Our immediate stunned reaction is that he has returned. But within seconds we realize what writer/director Benton is doing. As the camera pans the parishioners, we see Will and then Edna's children and then Edna, who passes the communion plate to the man next to her, who is her husband. He then passes the plate to the man next to him, who is Wiley, the black man who accidentally killed him. Writer/director Benton has given us a brilliant surrealistic celebration of the Eucharist, the meal that touches the deepest places in the heart and heals all wounds and injuries, and even conquers death.

The power and beauty of the three films, *Shane, On the Waterfront,* and *Places in the Heart* can be experienced by any audience. Each film in a different way can challenge our consciences, expand and deepen our worldview, help us to see more deeply into the human mystery and also into the Divine Mystery. These films, and many others, can be channels of Revelation. Some films are a treasure waiting to be discovered and re-discovered again and again.

CONCLUSION

An Encompassing Spirituality

EACH person has a story. The essence of each person's story is being written by the person's free choices and God's unlimited love. God's love and the human person's free choices create the person to be who he or she is. Every person's story is more wonderful, marvelous, and blessed than any individual can appreciate or even comprehend completely. Because of God's presence, every person's story is a love story.

Though Pope Francis' terminology is different than the philosophers, theologians, and religious thinkers I have generously borrowed from in writing this book—thinkers such as Michael Himes, John Haught, W. Norris Clarke, S.J., Andrew Greeley, Gabriel Marcel, Joannes Metz, Peter Quinn, Gerard Manley Hopkins, S.J., James Martin, S.J., Gordon Kaufman, Richard Viladesau, Francis X. Durrwell, C.SS.R, Michael Paul Gallagher, S.J., Karl Rahner, S.J., Hans Urs von Balthasar, Emmanuel Mounier, Bernard Lonergan, S.J., John Courtney Murray, S.J., Walker Percy, Flannery O'Connor, Edmond J. Dunn, Graham Greene, Evelyn Waugh, Ron Hansen and Lloyd Baugh, S.J.,—he presents basically the same view of the human person that all these thinkers seem to hold. This may not be too surprising since all but one of the thinkers are Catholic and several are Jesuits. What the Holy Father does through his spirituality of poverty is to focus the meaning and mystery of the human person on the person's dependence in being on God and the person's dependence for redemption on God. Pope Francis' emphasis on encouraging all of us to remember the poor highlights that Christian love is powerful. We receive the power to love through Jesus' Incarnation and we should express that love by reaching through the gift of self to those less fortunate than we. Especially interesting is the Pope's encouragement that we personally deal with the poor, not just through some charitable organization but as it were face-to-face or flesh to flesh as Jesus did.

Pope Francis' spirituality of poverty of the spirit may lead to a rebirth among large numbers of Catholics and also among a large number of those who are not Catholic. It could mark the coming of a "second spring" for the Catholic Church. I hope it will.